BE BRAVE

COURAGE FOR TODAY

Steve and Marjie Schaefer

ISBN: 979-8-9909136-2-2
Cover Design: Lisa McKenney
Interior Layout and Design: Kristi Knowles

Watch, stand fast in the faith, be brave, be strong. Let all that you do be done with love.

1 Corinthians 16:13-14

Table of Contents

Introduction

"Wait patiently for the Lord, be brave and courageous,
yes, wait patiently for the Lord" (Psalm 27:14).

What does it mean to *be brave?* The famous actor John Wayne once summed it up this way, "Courage is being scared to death and saddling up anyway."

Can you relate? Have you ever faced something that required a considerable amount of courage, and the only solution was to move toward the very adversary opposing you? We've all been there. Life seems to have a knack for boxing us into a corner, leaving us with no option but the one less traveled. Going towards the very thing that scares us to death. Fortunately, few days are so intense, although most days require bravery just to get out of bed.

Now, Google is replete with amazing quotes about bravery, and there are many Pinterest-worthy pithy quotes that are very inspirational in our quest for it. But when push comes to shove, all these sayings won't do the deed for us. There comes a time when we need to saddle up and just do it. So, what can we do to cultivate courage in our own lives *before* the inevitable comes?

Certainly, countless examples of brave people could spur us on. The Bible is filled with them, and we will study them in the days ahead. But at the end of the day, Marjie and I honestly believe the surest way to be brave is to live a life based on the promises of the Word of God and the constant clinging to the abiding presence of the Holy Spirit.

Yes, His presence is our confidence. Not only with us, but in us. As we trust His Word, He gives grace upon grace for every challenge we might face, and the assurance He will never leave us or forsake us. But how will we know all of this if we do not open his living and active Word for ourselves, and discover the supernatural provision He alone can provide?

If we were to encapsulate this supernatural provision in an image, we don't think we could have done a better job than what Lisa captured for us on our cover. The open sea is like life, sometimes tranquil but more often turbulent. Without shelter stronger than the winds and waves, we frail humans would be destined for a watery grave. But then we run to our Lighthouse, and hidden in Christ we now confidently declare, *"You are my hiding place; You shall preserve me from trouble; You shall surround me with songs of deliverance" (Psalm 32:7),* right smack dab in the middle of the storm. This is a courage not our own, for *"God is our refuge and strength, a very present help in trouble, therefore we will not fear"* (Psalm 46-1-2).

As C. S. Lewis once said, "Courage is not simply one of the virtues, but the form of every virtue at the testing point." That's how crucial bravery is in the Christian life. So let's do this. Let's dive into His Word and be brave together!

Christic In Us
Our Source

"Then Judas, having received a detachment of troops....
came there with lanterns, torches, and weapons.
Jesus therefore, knowing all things that would come
upon Him, went forward..." (John 18:3-4).

"Christ in you, the hope of glory"
(Colossians 1:27).

"I have come,' said a deep voice behind them.
They turned and saw the Lion himself, so bright and
real and strong that everything else began at once to
look pale and shadowy compared with him."

C.S. Lewis, *The Silver Chair*

Our Source

Good role models are essential in life. In fact, this book has many writings devoted to such heroes of the faith, inspirational examples we all can aspire to emulate. And yet, those folks from the past can't help us today. Good examples can't hold our hand in the storm, nor can we hide behind them as *they* bravely face the opposing force intended for us. Whether we like it or not, that ball is squarely in our court alone. We'd like them to, but unfortunately, role models can't empower us to move toward our Goliaths rather than away, stand alone when others have fled, or valiantly resist when others are waving the white flag of surrender. No, for these moments, we need much more. An inner strength not our own. Resilience not our own. A power not our own. We need Jesus.

And not Jesus the good example or Jesus the role model, although He's obviously both. Instead, we'll need something far more supernatural. Yes, His presence with us, but also His presence *in* us. The experience of an exchanged life—ours for His, death for life, weakness for strength, fear for faith. We need an intervention.

Despite many misconceptions to the contrary, virtue and morality do not make the Christian life. Habitation does. Supernatural habitation of Christ in the Person of the Holy Spirit. Having been born again by God, that very same God, the One who courageously endured the cross… He began living in you. Incomprehensible as it may seem, your physical body is now a host of our Living Savior, the Lord Jesus Christ.

And that is why brave Gladys Aylward would say, "…..my courage, only borrowed from Him." Gladys realized it wasn't her. Something else, or more accurately, Someone else, provided the inner ability to move forward despite the evil and opposition she so frequently encountered. Today, that same power which was in her is now in you. Like Gladys, you can. Why? Because He can. So come. Come to the living waters of Christ and discover this unfathomable strength and bravery not your own. Find courage for today.

"I have been crucified with Christ; it is no longer I who live, but Christ lives in me; and the life which I now live in the flesh I live by faith in the Son of God who loved me and gave Himself for me"
(Galatians 2:20).

The Answer

"That I may know Him and the power of His resurrection, and the fellowship of His sufferings, being conformed to His death" (Philippians 3:10).

Recently, I had breakfast with a friend, and as we talked about life and all its many problems and unanswered questions, I was reminded of a sign by the freeway where I live. In big neon letters, it says *Jesus Is The Answer*. Why was I reminded of that sign? Because we kept returning to Him. The person of Christ. But what struck me most about that conversation was what we did *not* keep coming back to.

We did not keep coming back to a formulaic solution. Do these three things, and you'll have your answer. We did not keep defaulting to an algorithm. If you do this, then God will do that. And we did not go to morality—the dos and don'ts of life. If you perform the following religious duties perfunctorily, you'll appease and satisfy your stern Father, earning His favor and guaranteeing smooth passage ahead. No, ultimately, the destination we kept arriving at was not morality, virtue, activity, or effort. In fact, it wasn't even Christianity, one of many sitting on the shelf of world religions. The answer we kept coming back to was a Person. The Person of Jesus Christ.

Surprisingly, when Thomas wanted to know the destination, Jesus only pointed him in one direction. Himself. *"I am the way, the truth, and the life. No one comes to the Father except through Me"* (John 14:6). In response to those loaded down with weighty problems, Christ's solution was again Himself, *"Come to Me, all you who labor and are heavy laden, and I will give you rest"* (John 11:28). And in the final words He chose to speak before He ascended, we see this pattern yet again, *"Lo, I am with you always, even to the end of the age"* (Matthew 28:20).

So yes, in bold neon letters, *Jesus Is The Answer.* There may be no immediate fix to your difficult dilemma, no quick solution, or speedy responses to life's unanswered questions. But He will be there. And finding Him in the mess of it all, ongoing communion and trust in Jesus will be His answer for you.

The End

"In Your presence is fullness of joy" (Psalm 16:11).

In the complexities and difficulties of life, it's hard to remain focused on our ultimate end. The end, that is, according to God. For here, we constantly have all sorts of gaps between our present experience and our preferred state. So we pray, asking God to bring about what we want and desire. God being the means to our end. For the unmarried, it may be a spouse. For the childless, a child. For the unemployed, a job. For the sick, health. For the hungry, food. And the Bible encourages us to pray for these very things. Our merciful God is pleased when we do. And yet, in the end, are the answers the end? For us, yes. But for God? What is His end?

To answer, we need go no farther than the two commissions given by God to His people. The first to Israel, and the second to Christ's disciples. One the shadow, and the other the reality. One Canaan, and the other the world. And in both instances, what were God's final words? In both, His final words were relational. *"...for the Lord your God is with you wherever you go"* (Joshua 1:9), and *"...and lo, I am with you always, even to the end of the age"* (Matthew 28:20). We've been commissioned to go, and go we ought, and yet could the going merely be the means to an end? The end being....... Him.

From a human perspective, we see God as a means to our end. And in a very real way, He is. Only God can answer our prayers. And yet, might the greater reality be the opposite of our human logic? Might the true gap be intimacy with Christ? This was Paul's conclusion as he sat in his gap, a Roman dungeon, and declared the startling endgame of his life. Not his release from prison, but *"that I may know Him and the power of His resurrection, and the fellowship of His sufferings, being conformed to His death"* (Philippians 3:10).

For, in the end, your greatest reality is not here but there. And in heaven, what is our end? The person of Jesus Christ. *"He will dwell with them, and they shall be His people. God Himself will be with them and be their God. And God will wipe away every tear from their eyes" (*Revelation 21:3-4). So here, let's press into Christ with every fiber of our being, and declare as Paul, *"For me to live is Christ, and to die is gain"* (Philippians 1:21).

What's Love Got to Do with It?

"For God has not given us a spirit of fear, but of power and of love and of a sound mind" (2 Timothy 1:7).

Language is a funny thing. In America, our primary language is English. A common language ensures communication between individuals and for society as a whole. Or does it? Take, for instance, the following. One exclaims, "That video game is so *awesome*!" while another states, "God is awesome." One declares, "I *love* Flaming Hot Doritos," while another shares, "I love Jesus." Same words. Two very different meanings. We all speak a foreign language, each to the other. No wonder there's so much misunderstanding.

Take, for instance, Tina Turner. She belted out, *"What's love, but a second-hand emotion."* Really? I beg to differ. In the above verse from 2 Timothy, the word *"love"* in Greek is *agape*. Unconditional, sacrificial love. A love that compels one to do anything for another, up to and including sacrificing themselves, without expecting anything in return. That is *agape*, and that is the love we receive from God in Christ. And that love is far greater than any second-hand emotion. It's a love equipping us to defeat the one thing that will kill our courage and bravery: Fear.

In fact, the Apostle John said it explicitly: *"perfect love [agape] casts out fear"* (1 John 4:18). The opposite of fear is <u>not</u> courage. The opposite of fear is agape. And so, you know that spirit of fear that wants to suffocate you and make you anxious over a million horrible scenarios that might happen? It's not from God. What, then, is from God? Love is. His agape for us and in us. So, given we empower what we focus on, will we focus on (mentally, emotionally, and verbally) what we fear, or will we focus on our God and His love for us? Will we be like the army of Israel, consumed with the size of Goliath, or will we be like David, who magnified His God? The choice is ours to make.

In the end, the source of your bravery is the person of Jesus. This intimacy with Christ enabled Paul to continually place his fears at the foot of the cross, to the point where he could declare, *"I am persuaded that neither death nor life, nor angels nor principalities, nor powers, nor things present nor things to come, nor height nor depth nor any other created things, shall be able to separate us from the love of God which is in Christ Jesus our Lord"* (Romans 8:38-39).

It seems love has everything to do with it.

He Waited Patiently

"God waited patiently while Noah was building his boat" (1 Peter 3:20).

I can count on one hand the number of times a DIY project went precisely according to plan. On time, on budget, with no hiccups. With 100's of projects under my belt, it typically begins with something to this effect, "Honey, I'll be done in a couple of hours." Famous last words. What then occurs is some combination of the following: I don't have the right tool(s), the part doesn't fit, the color isn't right, I cut myself, the hammer crushes my finger, the hardware store doesn't have what I need, and if it does, I chose the wrong one, so back I go. HGTV makes it look so easy.

So here we have Noah. He's tasked with the greatest DIY project ever given to mankind. Build a boat so large it will save humanity and all living creatures. Quite the undertaking. One guy. No Amazon, no Home Depot, no DeWalt, and no hydraulics. God could have done it differently. He could have spoken the boat into existence. He could have built it Himself or conscripted thousands of laborers to do the job. But no, He chose one man to do the job. And then He waited. And waited. And waited. One day at a time. And I'm sure there were days when things didn't progress as planned. The piece of wood didn't fit. The mallet broke. Noah had an on-the-job injury involving L&I and had to take a few weeks off from work. And yet, through it all, *"God waited patiently."*

How amazing and good our Lord is. He is what He requires. He practices what He preaches. With every character quality God exhorts us to display, He has first shown us by both essence and example. Here, God waited patiently for Noah, and now He exhorts us to do the same: *"Be still before the Lord and wait patiently for Him"* (Psalm 37:7).

So as you live out this life of faith, may you do so in communion with Him, abiding in Christ so His attributes might be your fruit, a by-product of *"Christ in you, the hope of glory"* (Colossians 1:27). His *"love, joy, peace, patience, kindness, goodness, faithfulness, gentleness, and self-control"* (Galatians 5:22-23). The fruit of a life hidden in Jesus.

Christly Throughout

"For I know that my Redeemer lives, and He shall stand at last on the earth"
(Job 19:25).

Throughout the history of Christianity, there have been teachers who have espoused (erroneously) the irrelevancy of the Old Testament for the believer, thinking it unnecessary and decoupling it from the New. And yet, this would be akin to writing a biography without including one's formative upbringing. In telling the entire story, every chapter is necessarily and organically tied to the other. Any first-time reader of the New Testament would naturally inquire, "Aren't we missing something here? Where's the first half of this story?" For all the Old is organically connected to the New, pointing forward to the coming Christ.

Take, for instance, the book of Job. Generally regarded as the oldest book in the Old Testament, Job deals with pain and suffering. A lot of it. A good life suddenly struck with many calamities. From every side. Bad and getting worse". Not a book we generally turn to when we need a pick-me-up. But even here, we see the coming Messiah and Job's dependency upon Him.

Initially feeling abandoned and forsaken by God amid his pain, Job cries out, *"If only there were someone to mediate between us* [Job and God]*, someone to bring us together"* (Job 9:33). Then one of his buddies reminds him of the dilemma we all face, *"Get rid of your sins, and leave all iniquity behind you"* (Job 11:14). In response, Job recognizing this impossibility, turns to Jesus his Redeemer and declares, by faith, hope in Him and his physical resurrection:

> *"For I know that my Redeemer lives, and He shall stand at last on the earth. And after my skin is destroyed, this I know, that in my flesh I shall see God, whom I shall see for myself, and my eyes shall behold, and not another. How my heart yearns within me!"* (Job 19:25-27).

Our hope was Job's hope. Christ in the Old. Christ in the New. Christ everywhere. So let us dwell in the Old as we do the New, and find the treasure of Jesus Christ throughout.

What if we were brave, instead?

"To all who mourn in Israel, He will give a crown of beauty for ashes, a joyous blessing instead of mourning, festive praise instead of despair. Instead of shame and dishonor, you will enjoy a double share of honor" (Isaiah 61:3, 7).

Did you know Jesus had a life purpose statement? It's Isaiah 61. Written in the first person (verses 1, 8, 10), this chapter reveals His expressed purpose in coming to earth and the fruit from it. Why don't you read it now? It's found, in part, in Luke 4:18-19, where Jesus stands up in a synagogue and reads from Isaiah 61. After sitting down, to paraphrase, He says, "That's Me." In this section of Scripture from Isaiah, two things stand out. First, Jesus came to bring God's favor, enabling us by His Spirit to live in expectancy of God's goodness. And second, He offers us a keyword in His life purpose. The word *"instead."* In giving us Jesus Christ, His Son, God has given us an alternative to what has gone on and is going on in our lives. If we are up against the enemy of our soul, Jesus has something else for us *instead*.

Instead of mourning, He gives us a joyous blessing. Instead of despair, He gives us festive praise. And instead of shame and dishonor, He gives us a double share. This is divine displacement. God coming into our lives with such power and such display, that He displaces everything the enemy has stored in our lives. Life has dealt each of us difficulty, disillusionment, disappointment, discouragement, despair, and flat-out disasters, but Jesus came to earth to displace all these realities with a greater reality. Himself.

The life purpose of Jesus addresses the very parts of your life that haven't worked and aren't working now. What if we could discover that God always backs us up 100% with His goodness? What if instead of frustration with how things aren't working in our lives, we learn that Jesus is setting us up for something else…. instead? What if, instead of fear, we tapped into His courage?

What if we were brave, instead?

Alive With Him

"And you... being dead He has made alive, having wiped out the handwriting of requirements that was against us...having nailed it to the cross. Having disarmed principalities and powers, He made a public spectacle of them, triumphing over them in it" (Colossians 2:13-15).

We all have things in our lives the enemy has thrown at us. We all have "stuff," and perhaps we've stored some of it away. Things like fear, insecurity, rejection, offenses, disappointment, and heartache. They pile up, and we think we'll deal with them one day, but for now, we hide them away, and they begin to create a mess. Kind of like a closet over the years. Things accumulate, and someday, we'll clean and organize it. But that day never comes. So we just shut the door.

We can sometimes live like this spiritually, too. Things accumulate, things we haven't dealt with, stuffing the hurt deep into our souls. This spiritual storage closet twists our perspective of who we are, convincing us we do not belong, do not matter, or that our lives are inconsequential. Which often leads to fear, dread, or anxiety. When we believe these things, we end up accommodating the enemy. And when we do that, we invite the enemy in, for believing the lie empowers the liar.

And this is why we have the life message of Jesus in Isaiah 61. We have become the recipients of His life purpose. Jesus has empowered us to move from just mentally assenting to God's love to receiving it. This is what Isaiah 61 is all about. It's about our *insteads*. It's about our heritage of divine displacement. These verses are reminders to focus on the promises of Jesus and not on the messy closet of our past.

When something difficult comes against us, we have a choice. We have an instead. We can focus on what happened or is happening, or we can become preoccupied with our *instead*. Jesus has already removed anything coming against us and has nailed it to the cross! No weapon formed against us shall prosper. Our passion for the goodness of God and living from a place of expectancy enables us to shake it off, look for the blessing, and align our lives with His goodness. And it's this goodness that enables us to be brave.

Feeling Invisible

"And whatever you do, do it heartily, as to the Lord and not to men,
knowing that from the Lord you will receive the reward of the inheritance;
for you serve the Lord Christ" (Colossians 3:23-24).

Feeling invisible to others can be one of the most discouraging things we face in life. This form of rejection makes us feel devalued, birthing a sense of worthlessness compared to the value we see in others. Like when the person you are talking with keeps looking over your shoulder, desperately searching for someone far more interesting or important to talk to. Or that feeling you get when in a group, you speak up, only to have your comments ignored after a long and awkward silence. These moments in time make us feel isolated, severed from the relational connections we were created to have.

While this sense of invisibility can be so painful (and yet used by Him to draw us closer to Himself), there is another invisibility we can purely and more easily rejoice in—the invisibility of an invisible job well done. There are many things in life that, if done with a spirit of excellence, will go completely unnoticed by others. Like dishes magically ending up in the dishwasher. Carpets that somehow aren't dirty. Chairs that miraculously set themselves up. Green grass that seemingly never grows. Garbage that mysteriously disappears. And refrigerators with always an ample supply of milk.

Consider, for a moment, referees or umpires in a sporting event. If they do their job, you don't really notice them. But blow a call, and that's all anyone is talking about the next day. Or consider your grocery store. We take for granted that there will always be oranges sitting there, never realizing the oranges you are looking at today were in a different country the last time you shopped.

Yes, so much of life was designed by God to be anonymous. Never to be seen, recognized, or lauded by the world or people around us. In fact, in many ways and at many times, you are that referee in life. Excelling in your invisible results. And that's ok. Because Jesus always sees. Your audience of One.

Bent But Not Broken

"A bent reed He will not break off, and a dimly burning wick He will not extinguish, until He leads justice to victory. And in His name the Gentiles will hope"
(Matthew 12:20-21).

In football, there is a defensive scheme called *bend, but don't break*. Basically, it says in the era of high-powered, Air Raid college offenses (that's where they pass the ball a lot vs. run), this defensive alignment will rush four linemen, with the rest playing in zones. The goal is to keep all the plays in front of them, not to allow any big plays. To limit the damage. The idea is eventually, the offense will be stopped, and the opposing team will have to settle for a field goal attempt. When a *bend but don't break* approach is executed according to plan, the defense may appear broken to the spectators in the stands, but in the end, the opposing force is halted, and the defense comes off the field having gained the victory.

Do you ever feel like you're living a *bend but don't break* kind of life? Overwhelmed with responsibilities, weary of the problems, carrying the weight of the world upon your shoulders? Especially when you experience a convergence zone of difficulties and troubles with the people and circumstances in your life. From your vantage point, you're broken, shattered, helpless, humbled, surrendered, and hopeless. From His? You're bent. *Surely, it can't get any worse*, you think, only to discover it does. But you awake the following day to discover that, by God's grace, you could bend just a little bit more.

 As life bends you, turn to Jesus. He promises not to break you. In fact, quite the opposite:

> *"Come to Me, all you who labor and are heavy laden, and I will give your rest. Take My yoke upon you and learn from Me, for I am gentle and lowly of heart, and you will find rest for your souls. For My yoke is easy and My burden is light"* (Matthew 11:28-30).

Yes, go to Jesus. Why? Because He cares for you, so cast all your cares upon Him. You may be weary, but Jesus never grows weary of you. Come boldly to His throne of grace and receive His mercy to help in your time of need. By doing so in the game of life, you, too, in the end, will come off the field victorious.

Students For Life

"Instruct the wise, and they will be wiser still; teach the righteous, and they will add to their learning" (Proverbs 9:9).

In April of 1972, Alice Cooper released the smash hit *School's Out*, an anthem for many years for all students escaping school on that glorious first day of summer vacation. While the song promised *"school's out forever"* and *"we might not come back at all,"* the summer would go by quickly, and the bulk of us would return in September. So much for the euphoria of June.

While the realm of formal education here on earth will eventually end, in the realm of the eternal, it never will. For us mortals, there is no graduation ceremony, no playing of *Pomp and Circumstance,* just a transfer portal from this earthly dimension to heaven. So, until then, we will always be learning. Here, we will always be students. Whether nine or ninety, there is so much more to know about our immortal and infinite God:

> *"Oh, the depth of the riches both of the wisdom and knowledge of God! How unsearchable are His judgments and His ways past finding out!"* (Romans 11:33).

Two kings of Judah thought otherwise. Having faithfully walked with God for many years, near the end of their earthly existence, both thought they knew it all, resisting input from others. King Joash rejected the prophet Zechariah's call to turn back to the Lord and murdered God's messenger instead (2 Chronicles 24:17-25). And King Uzziah, whose pride created a stubborn heart and ears refusing to hear, which led to his leprosy until his dying day (2 Chronicles 26:16-21). Two kings who began with teachable spirits ended up otherwise as they approached the finish line of life.

To the aged and those soon to be, may we never lose our love of learning in all matters pertaining to the Lord. *"For of Him and through Him and to Him are all things, to whom be glory forever. Amen"* (Romans 11:36).

The Pit of Despair

"I waited patiently for the Lord to help me, and He turned to me and heard my cry. He lifted me out of the pit of despair, out of the mud and mire" (Psalm 40:1-2).

The Princess Bride is a 1987 classic romantic adventure movie complete with true love, the "inconceivable," and a dungeon aptly named the Pit of Despair. Here, our hero, Westley, awakens to find himself strapped to *The Machine* while an odd-looking albino stands over him, tending to his wounds. "Where am I?" Westley demands. "The Pit of Despair," the albino replies in a raspy, menacing voice – before clearing his throat and continuing the conversation in a perfectly normal British accent. Poor Westley is in a horrible predicament, for Count Rugen is about to apply his diabolical torturing methods upon him. But alas – spoiler alert – Westley escapes, overcomes a few obstacles, and is reunited with his true love, Buttercup. And they lived happily ever after. The End.

The Oxford Dictionary defines *despair* as "a feeling of having lost all hope." Haven't we all felt that at one time or another? Maybe you're feeling it right now. Life closes in, and the perfect storm of circumstances aligns to render you hopeless about life and the future. David was there. He was in a pit of despair. Psalm 40 is his description of that experience and how God rescued him. But first, he had to wait. That seemingly excruciating, eternal wait. Then God did what God does. He turned to him. He heard him. He lifted him up, and his hope and joy returned. And now, David's unchanging God is your God, and as you humble yourself before Him, He promises to *"exalt you in due time, casting all your care upon Him, for He cares for you"* (I Peter 5:6-7).

Like Westley and, more importantly, David, you also will escape the pit. He *will* lift you up. For your True Love is with you, He cares for you, and He is able to do far more than we can ask or imagine. Even now, He says to you, *"In the world you will have tribulation; but be of good cheer, I have overcome the world"* (John 16:33).

> *"May the God of all grace, who called us to His eternal glory by Christ Jesus, after you have suffered a while, perfect, establish, strengthen, and settle you. To Him be the glory and the dominion forever and ever. Amen"* (1 Peter 5:10-11).

What do you see?

"The eye is the lamp of the body. If your eyes are healthy,
your whole body will be full of light"(Matthew 6:22-23).

Thought experiment. If I placed a glass in front of you, what would you see: A glass half full or a glass half empty? Both answers would be correct. And yet, I daresay, what you see and how you respond will reveal quite a bit about how you view the world and your life in it. Consider the following:

Some grumble at why God put thorns on roses. Others notice, with awe and wonder, that God has put roses among the thorns.

Nancy DeMoss Woglemuth shares the following story:

> "Steve Dale, a syndicated columnist who answers people's questions about their pets, received an email from a reader seeking advice regarding her twelve-year-old boxer that was at risk of losing one leg to a cancerous tumor. Dale responded that three-legged dogs actually adjust fairly quickly after surgery and are soon getting around nearly as well as before. 'The psychological trauma of being expected to feel sad because they've lost a limb just doesn't seem to occur. Instead, quite the reverse, they act overjoyed to be alive.'"

On July 30, 1967, 17-year-old Joni Eareckson Tada dove into the Chesapeake Bay. Misjudging the depth of the water, she fractured her cervical vertebrae and became a quadriplegic. Today, she states, "My weakness, that is my quadriplegia, is my greatest asset, because it forces me into the arms of Christ every single morning when I get up."

And from the depths of a Roman prison, Paul writes, *"Rejoice in the Lord always. Again I will say rejoice. Indeed I have all and abound. I am full"* (Philippians 4:4,18).

Thorns, a missing leg, quadriplegia, prison. Roses, three legs, Christ, abundance. What do you see?

Best Listen to Paul

"But the officers in charge of the prisoners listened more to the ship's captain and the owner than to Paul" Acts 27:11).

I like experts. Especially when my engine light is on, I have a complicated tax issue, my laptop is dead, or I need brain surgery. Without human experts, I suspect my life would be in complete shambles in a short span of time. So God bless people who specialize in what they do. We need their expertise!

That said, there's wisdom to be gleaned from this passage in the Book of Acts. Paul has been arrested and is about to be shipped off to Rome, where he will stand trial before Caesar. But given the time of year, *"... sailing was now dangerous"* (Acts 27:9), Paul warned the decision makers they shouldn't do it (Acts 27:10). But did the centurion and soldiers listen to Paul? Of course not. They listened to the experts: The ship's captain and the owner of the ship. I'm sure these were grizzled maritime authorities, well acquainted with the things of the sea. The tentmaker Paul? Not so much. What did he know about sailing? But, as it turns out, Paul was right. Tempests and storms blew, and the expedition would soon become a shipwreck with catastrophic loss of property.

Remarkably, however, everyone on board would live. Why? Because the centurion and soldiers had learned their lesson. *"Paul said to the centurion and the soldiers, 'Unless these men* [the sailors] *stay in the ship, you cannot be saved.' Then the soldiers cut away the ropes of the skiff and let it fall off"* (Acts 27:31). They now listened to Paul, and as a result, all crew members survived.

This is the same Paul whom God would use to write thirteen books of the New Testament. Yes, while experts are excellent and necessary, God is the Source of all their expertise. He is the Expert of experts. So, unlike the desperate centurion and his soldiers, let's not wait until we've exhausted every other option, making God our last resort. Instead, let's turn to Him and His Word *first*, just as Jesus did when faced with the trials (Matthew 26:36-46) and temptations (Matthew 4:1-11) of His life. In doing so, we'll find He's quite capable, as our Captain, to bring life's voyage safely to port.

Compartmentalizing God

"Now Solomon brought the daughter of Pharaoh up from the City of David to the house he had built for her, for he said, 'My wife shall not dwell in the house of David king of Israel, because the places to which the ark of the Lord has come are holy'"
(2 Chronicles 8:11).

Each room in a house serves a critical yet unique function. And within one particular room, the kitchen, each drawer and cabinet serves a similar organizing purpose. I guess home builders could create one big dumping ground for all things kitchen-related, but I suspect those houses wouldn't sell. No, we need these separate compartments to help us maintain some semblance of order. Utensils go here, pots and pans go there, and cookie sheets go in the drawer under the oven.

However, what works for the kitchen does not work in our relationship with the Lord. In today's verse, we read about Solomon, the wisest man on earth (1 Kings 10:23), who would one day end his life distant from God. How come? Because of his foreign wives, and how they *"turned his heart after other gods; and his heart was not loyal to the Lord his God"* (1 Kings 11:4). Yet he knew. He knew it wasn't right to marry this *"daughter of Pharaoh,"* so he built a separate home for her, far, far away from the holy presence of the Lord.

How interesting, just four verses later, we read, *"Solomon did not deviate in any way from David's commands concerning the priests and Levites and the treasuries"* (2 Chronicles 8:15). In one compartment, he deviated, and in another, he did not. Let Solomon's life be a warning to us all. To act and speak one way at work or with friends on a night out, and yet quite another at church on Sunday, reveals a Solomon-like mindset to life. Compartmentalization is great for our homes and in the kitchen, but foolish in our relationship with Jesus Christ. He is the Lord of the entire manor, and as such, He has full reign and authority to rule 24/7 in every room (and drawer) of our house, His home.

One Step at a Time

"A man's heart plans his way, but the Lord directs his steps" (Proverbs 16:9).

"So, what's the plan?" We all want to know what the plan is. What will we do, and where will we go with this, that, or the other thing. Troops want to know the battle plan. Players want to see the game plan. Amazon sells a wide array of Daily Planners, and we often ask, "Do you have any vacation plans for the summer?" Humans are planners by nature. Given the chaos constantly swirling about, plans give us a sense of order and hope, providing clarity of direction as we charge into the foggy future.

But how do we respond when our plans go awry? Do we hit the curve ball, or do we strike out? It's at this juncture where we've all seen a variety of responses kick in. Do we recalibrate our plans accordingly, or do we begin to control or manipulate the people and circumstances in our lives to reestablish those original plans? We've all witnessed, experienced, or maybe even have been the controller at one time or another. Imposing and tightening our grip upon those around us as we see our initial plan going astray. Or the manipulator, who refuses to adapt, wedded to their agenda, whether hidden or visible.

The dilemma with God's *"directs his steps"* approach is it requires trust. Faith in Him. Because like it or not, we only take one step at a time, whereas a plan has many steps laid out into the future. For if we really believe the Lord sovereignly directs our steps, can we trust Him for steps 2, 3, 4, and beyond? And therein lies the rub. Trusting Him. We want to know all the steps all at once. But that's not how we walk, and that's not how the Lord typically reveals Himself.

So go ahead and plan, but understand He reveals His direction as we go. With open hands with our plan, know that He... and not our plan... is our order and hope for the future. One step at a time.

Follow the Leader

"Imitate me, just as I also imitate Christ" (1 Corinthians 11:1).

Leaders and leadership come in all shapes and sizes. We typically think of it in terms of a formal capacity, the kind that possesses true authority in directing others. However, leaders can also be informal, who, through wisdom and competency, lead others via their influence. While attention is primarily given to those in formal leadership roles, informal leaders often exert the most profound and lasting influence on others. Regardless, whether formal or informal, leaders disproportionately affect the world around them.

We see it above in the Apostle Paul, instructing the church in Corinth (and us) to follow him as he follows Christ. We see it in Hezekiah, the King of Judah, who *"who humbled himself and repented of his pride...,"* and his followers responded in kind, *"... as did the people of Jerusalem"* (2 Chronicles 32:26). Or David, who gave all his private treasures of gold and silver to the building of the Temple and asked, *"Who will follow my example and give offerings to the Lord today?"* (1 Chronicles 29:5), and in response the people *"all gave willingly...and rejoiced over the offerings, for they had given freely and wholeheartedly to the Lord"* (v. 6, 9). Leaders have the responsibility to use their disproportionate influence to do good, pointing others to Jesus Christ.

Unfortunately, leaders have this same power and impact to spread evil, too. And in the church today, we've had far too many examples of shepherds eating versus protecting their sheep. So whether we are called to lead or to follow, we are called to do so as Christ. So let's lead as Jesus does His church, and follow as Christ did His Father while about His earthly ministry. Unlike the world's chain of command, we lead and follow under Jesus Christ, for ours is a chain of submission:

> *"Obey those who rule over you, and be submissive, for they watch out for your souls, as those who must give account. Let them do so with joy and not grief, for that would be unprofitable for you"* (Hebrews 11:17).

I'll See It When I Believe It

"And whatever things you ask in prayer, believing, you will receive"
(Matthew 21:22).

My sense is God gave every human being a level of skepticism regarding our beliefs. Which I suspect He provided as an innate safeguard against every whim or delusional idea we may conjure up or come our way. Our propensity towards doubt and suspicion acts as a healthy and necessary protection against deception and being led astray. That's why *I'll believe it when I see it.*

Two individuals in the Bible typify this mindset. The first is the queen of Sheba, who could not fathom Solomon was as wise as everyone said. But after seeing Solomon and listening to him, she changed her tune, *"I didn't believe what was said until I arrived here and saw it with my own eyes"* (2 Chronicles 9:6). And the other being the disciple Thomas. While all the other disciples were excitedly sharing about seeing the risen Jesus, doubting Thomas skeptically replied,

> *"Unless I see in His hands the print of the nails, and put my finger into the print of the nails and put my hand into His side, I will not believe"* (John 20:25).

And then along came Jesus—to the Thomas in all of us. He chose us, called us out of darkness, gave us faith, and gifted us His Spirit and written Word—and all the promises therein. *"For we walk by faith, not by sight"* (2 Corinthians 5:7).

So now, when it comes to God and what He has spoken, do we trust Him? Do we believe what He said? Do we believe He is trustworthy? Do we believe *"... He is, and that He is a rewarder of those who diligently seek Him"* (Hebrews 11:6)? Is He, and his Word, worthy of this level of faith, trust, and belief? Independent, and oftentimes despite, what we see?

The answer to all these questions comes straight from Jesus Himself. Replying to our friend Thomas, a proxy for the skeptic in all of us, He said,

> *"Thomas, because you have seen Me, you have believed. Blessed are those who have not seen yet have believed"* (John 20:29).

Senior Moments

"Likewise you younger people, submit yourselves to your elders. Yes, all of you be submissive to your elders. Yes, all of you be submissive to one another and be clothed with humility, for 'God resists the proud, but gives grace to the humble'"
(1 Peter 5:5).

Senior moments seem to be a regular occurrence these days. What once was an isolated brain freeze now appears to be the new norm. Arriving at a room in the house only to wonder why I set out for that destination in the first place. Responding in conversation, but forgetting where I was going with my point. And the name... *"What's your name again?"* While these moments may be predominately reserved for the aged, the young have these moments, too. That is, moments when a senior is needed.

Rehoboam was such a young man. Having just taken over the reins of leadership from his father Solomon, a crucial decision lay before him. He had a choice. Do I listen to my dad's inner circle, or do I listen to my BFF's? Unfortunately, his gang provided the echo chamber he was looking for, rather than the contrarian input of wisdom: *"But Rehoboam rejected the advice of the older men and instead asked the opinion of the young men who had grown up with him and were now his advisors"* (2 Chronicles 10:8). Rejecting the advice of the old guys, he followed the counsel of his homies, and so began the divided kingdom and what would ultimately end in the demise of both.

Peer groups, YouTube, and Google are often poor substitutes for the wisdom that comes from experience. As our contemporary insurance tagline says, *"We know a thing or two because we've seen a thing or two."* While it may be new to you, for a senior, it's not their first rodeo.

And for young and old alike, may we all turn to Him in all our many senior moments, for *"Christ the power of God and the wisdom of God... Jesus, who became for us wisdom from God"* (1 Corinthians 1:24, 30). He alone is the One from which all true wisdom flows.

Our Force Field

"Be anxious for nothing, but in everything by prayer and supplication, with thanksgiving, let your requests be made known to God; and the peace of God, which surpasses all understanding, will guard your hearts and minds through Christ Jesus" (Philippians 4:6-7).

Wouldn't we all love to have a magic barrier we could immediately erect at the slightest hint of harm coming our way? Violet Parr did in the movie *The Incredibles*, possessing an ability to generate near-indestructible force fields to protect herself and others. And we all know Obi-Wan Kenobi had access to the force in *Star Wars* (although the purest might define this more as an energy field vs. a force field). And closer to the real world we have the Iron Dome, a mobile defense system designed to intercept short-range rockets endangering Israel.

As a believer in Christ, did you know you've actually been given such a defense? A supernatural blockade not requiring CGI or a billion-dollar contract with Rafael Advanced Defense Systems. Your invisible barrier guards your soul and flows into you as an outcome of the finished work of Jesus Christ and the pouring out of His Spirit into your heart (Romans 5:5). Your powerful peace from God *"will guard"* your heart and mind through Christ Jesus, while the shield of faith enables you *"to quench all the fiery darts of the wicked one"* (Ephesians 6:16). So like David, you can say:

"The Lord is my rock and my fortress and deliverer; my God, my strength, in whom I will trust; my shield and the horn of my salvation, my stronghold" (Psalm 18:2).

Yes, you've been given a protective wall for your soul no amount of money could ever build or Hollywood could ever produce. As Martin Luther wrote in *A Mighty Fortress*:

A mighty fortress is our God,
A bulwark never failing.

Attack! Retreat!

"Submit yourselves, then, to God. Resist the devil, and he will flee from you"
(James 4:7).

"Flee sexual immorality" (1 Corinthians 6:18).

God has drafted every Christian to fight in a war. No, not one with tanks, rifles, and grenades, but a spiritual war fought with spiritual weapons. Given this reality, whether we have served in the military or not, it behooves us to know some fundamental principles of war. Specifically, who is our enemy, and who is not? When do we fight, and when do we retreat? Defeat on the battlefield of life is pretty much guaranteed if we cannot accurately answer these most basic warfare questions.

In a nutshell, our enemy is the devil, the world, and our flesh. Notice I did not say spouse, boss, or that annoying person in the cubicle beside you. The Bible is clear: "... we *do not wrestle against flesh and blood"* (Ephesians 6:12), so let's rule out your co-worker and Aunt Beatrice as the problem. Instead, the passage says we're locked in a battle *"... against spiritual hosts of wickedness in the heavenly places"* (Ephesians 6:12b). So we fight the devil and do it with God's Word. Just as Jesus did when three times the devil tempted him in the desert (Matthew 4:1-11).

But that is *not* how we win against the flesh or the world. Here, a tactical retreat is in order. And this is where many of us get it all mixed up. Too many Christians run from the devil and fight the flesh when, in fact, the Bible says just the opposite. So when it comes to sexual immorality, pride, or the love of money, RUN!!

How do we discern who our enemy is at any given moment? Well, if it's the devil, here are his predictable calling cards: Condemnation (Romans 8:1), accusation (Revelation 12:10), lies (John 8:44), and anything associated with killing, stealing, or destroying you (John 10:10). And if it's the flesh or the world, here is the hand they typically play: Lust, pride (1 John 2:15-17), or greed (1 Timothy 6:10-12).

So let's accurately identify our true enemy and engage accordingly. In doing so, by God's grace, we will win the war we've been called to wage.

Call an Audible

"Give ear to my words, O Lord...Give heed to the voice of my cry...
My voice you shall hear in the morning, O Lord" (Psalm 5:1-3).

In football, when a team is going to run a play but decides at the last second to change it, they do what's called an audible at the line of scrimmage. An audible is a verbal instruction by the quarterback to slightly alter the predetermined play or scrap it for something else. What's interesting to note is the quarterback is not merely thinking of a different play, thereby leaving his other ten players in the dark, but is verbally instructing them what's going on in his mind as he scans the defense. It is, in fact, quite audible.

If you are like me, your quiet time with the Lord can be, well, very quiet. Makes me wonder if the term itself, *quiet time*, has served to influence our silence. Maybe. But I do see a disconnect when I compare and contrast it with the Bible and David's description of his time alone with Him. David does not request of God to "read my mind" or "give heed to my thoughts." And elsewhere, David says,

> *"But I will sing of Your power; yes, I will sing aloud of Your mercy in*
> *the morning; for You have been my defense and refuge in the day of*
> *my trouble" (Psalm 59:16).*

Of course, God can read our minds and know our thoughts. But that's missing the point. When we speak our prayers, sing to Him, and declare His promises out loud, we align and solidify the confession of our mouth with our mind. For

> *"... we have the same spirit of faith, according to what is written,*
> *'I believed and therefore I spoke,' we also believe and therefore*
> *speak" (2 Corinthians 4:13).*

While science is just now discovering the power of the audible word in strengthening our neural pathways, it seems the Bible and a lowly shepherd knew this truth thousands of years before.

God of the Mundane

"The Lord is more pleased when we do what is right and just than when we offer Him sacrifices" (Proverbs 21:3).

Non-profit ministries exist because of the generosity of others. Generous donors are the financial lifeblood of organizations formed to advance God's Kingdom here on earth. While these monetary sacrifices are all good and necessary, it is interesting to consider the relative weight God places on the Biblical scales of importance when it comes to sacrifice vs. obedience. While large donations and philanthropy will garner applause when high-dollar paddles are raised at a fundraising dinner, grab the headlines in your local paper, or get you a building dedicated in your name, obedience will most likely go unnoticed in the shadows of anonymity.

And isn't that just like our God? Coming to earth with no fanfare or hype, nothing going viral on social media, no reporters on-site with satellite connections, just some barn animals looking on as God inhabits their feeding trough. No one in Hollywood could have (or would have) written this script. It's too boring. It wouldn't sell. Yet this is how the King of Glory came to earth. So is it any surprise when He places a high priority on a cup of cold water? Or becomes ecstatic when a poor widow puts a couple of pennies in the offering plate? The apparently small and insignificant that fly under the radar. These are the actions so close to His heart.

As Samuel said to Saul after he had disobeyed the voice of the Lord,

> *"Has the Lord as great delight in burnt offerings and sacrifices, as in obeying the voice of the Lord? Behold, to obey is better than sacrifice"* (1 Samuel 15:22).

Obedience won't always get you into the limelight. You may or may not get a few pats on the back. But in the end, you will hear the only words that truly matter in all of life,

> *"Well done, good and faithful servant; you have been faithful over a few things. I will make you ruler over many things. Enter into the joy of your Lord"* (Matthew 25:23).

Whatever

"And whatever you do, do it heartily, as to the Lord and not to men"
(Colossians 3:23).

During a visit to the NASA Space Center in 1962, President Kennedy noticed a janitor, Joe Byerly, carrying a broom. He interrupted his tour, walked over to the man, and said: "Hi, I'm Jack Kennedy, what are you doing?" Joe responded: I'm helping put a man on the moon, Mr. President."

It's important to know your *why.*

Booker T Washington, when asked by Mrs. Ruffner to sweep a room at the Hampton Institute:

> "I swept the recitation room three times. Then I got a dusting cloth and dusted it four times. All the woodwork around the walls, every bench, table, and desk. I had the feeling that in large measure my future was dependent upon the impression I made upon the teacher in the cleaning of the room. When she was unable to find one bit of dirt on the floor, or a particle of dust on any of the furniture, she quietly remarked, 'I guess you will do to enter this institution.' I was one of the happiest souls on Earth. The sweeping of that room was my college examination, and never did any youth pass an examination for entrance into Harvard or Yale that gave him more genuine satisfaction."

It's important to excel in *how* you do your *what.*

While we may prioritize the quality of our effort based on the expected audience, the task's perceived importance, or how visible the final product will be, in Christ, in the final analysis, it's really all just for Him. He is our *why.* Our audience of One. Small or large. Visible or hidden. So let's embrace a spirit of excellence in *how* we do our *what,* *"... knowing that from the Lord you will receive the reward of the inheritance; for you serve the Lord Christ"* (Colossians 3:24).

A Shadow in the Night

"Though He slay me, yet I will hope in Him" (Job 13:15).

I became a new believer in the last half of my senior year in college, while I was right in the middle of my job hunt. Dreaming of a job in the financial industry since I was in high school, I was in the process of interviewing with a prestigious bank at the time. Door after door seemed to be swinging wide open for me, and I just knew this coveted job would be mine before I knew it. Besides, God was now on my side, so surely this thing was in the bag. Until which time I received the dreaded thin letter stating their rejection of me, and their wishes for a bright future. Somewhere else.

Suffice it to say, I pouted and was angry with God for days. My logical conditional statement of hypothesis and conclusion (If God loves me, then He will give me this job) had been utterly and catastrophically destroyed. A straight line had been drawn in my mind between God's eternal character and my tangible and desired outcome, and now that line had been obliterated.

In her book *The Night Is Normal*, Alicia Britt Chole eloquently delves into these experiences and our response(s) to them. Times such as these can create disillusionment in us towards God, causing our simplistic if/then beliefs about Him to be shattered. Destroyed by providential design. From Him.

> "So in the midst of our nights, when life breaks our if-thens into pieces, let us join Job in his loss and Jesus in His Gethsemane. When our logic proves itself too weak to hold reality, may we too lift our voices in prayer and say,
>
> > *I trust You, my God, more than I trust my understanding.*
> > *I want You, my Lord, more than I want to avoid pain.*
> > *I don't need sight to have faith.*
> > *I just need You.*
> > *So lead on, my Savior:*
> > *May my faith grow stronger within Your shadow."*

Home Sweet Home

"The voice of rejoicing and salvation is in the tents of the righteous" (Psalm 118:15).

What is home to you? God intended homes to be our happy place, a refuge where we can safely let our hair down, a haven for restoration and renewal, and a daily generator recharging us to return to that cold, cruel world we all must face. For me, home as an adult has been the *Hot Wheels* power station I once played with as a child. Losing power as my race car went around the orange track and its many loops; the power station was there in the nick of time to thrust my racer on to new land speed records.

That said, while home may be our private getaway from the world's insanity, it's foolish to think it lies secret from the Him who sees it all, for *"The Righteous One knows what is going on in the homes of the wicked"* (Proverbs 21:12). What's true of the wicked, is also true of the righteous. No home left behind!

Indeed, nothing is hidden from Him in our homes. All is open. All is visible. He has perfect vision of it all. And BTW, He has perfect hearing, too,

> *"Then they despised the pleasant land; they did not believe His word, but complained in their tents, and did not heed the voice of the Lord"* (Psalm 106:24-25).

We can't export what we don't have at home. So if we've stumbled in what He has seen or heard, let's receive His grace and forgiveness, seek reconciliation if need be, make our home His home, transparently welcoming Jesus into all our many activities and conversations, just as David welcomed Him in his,

> *"I will sing of mercy and justice; to You, O Lord, I will sing praises....*
> *I will walk within my house with a perfect heart. I will set nothing wicked before my eyes"* (Psalm 101:1-3).

Pardon Me

"Let the wicked forsake his way, and the unrighteous man his thoughts; let him return to the Lord, and He will have mercy on him; and to our God, for He will abundantly pardon" (Isaiah 55:7).

I've never spent time in prison, so I can't possibly appreciate what freedom must feel like after serving time. And getting out before the full sentence is served would seem, to me, to make any prisoner equally happy. Just get me out of here! But this only reveals my ignorance. For not all freedoms are alike. Take, for instance, being paroled vs. pardoned.

To be paroled is to be released conditionally, typically by a parole board, requiring the parolee to live within state and county lines, to meet regularly with a parole officer, submit to drug and alcohol tests, and provide proof of residence and employment. And the crime committed remains on your record. Forever.

In contrast, an unconditional pardon is typically only granted by the highest governmental official of their jurisdiction. The President if a federal crime was committed, or a Governor if it was a state offense. Unlike being paroled, a full pardon removes the consequences of a criminal conviction, wiping the slate clean and restoring rights lost due to the conviction. The guilty party is set free as though they were never convicted. As though it never even happened. Forever.

Unfortunately, it seems many Christians live as though we are on parole. Ruminating on past or present sins. Having a sense of being set free, but not entirely, due to perceived conditions. "I should attend church, read the Bible, and pray more. Be more patient, loving, and forgiving," to name just a few of the coulda, woulda, shoulda's. Do these, and you will maintain your freedom. Don't, and it's back to prison you go. But obligational living, in a misguided attempt to appease God, is a prison in and of itself.

But thanks be to God, we are not parolees. We have been fully pardoned. The Supreme Authority of the universe has granted us a complete and unconditional pardon by the finished work of Jesus Christ on the cross. Justice was served, the penalty was paid, and now we are the grateful recipients of His undeserved mercy. So rejoice, for *"if the Son sets you free, you will be free indeed"* (John 8:36).

The One Thing

"And the Lord said, 'Simon, Simon! Indeed, Satan has asked for you, that he may sift you as wheat. But I have prayed for you, that your faith should not fail… "
(Luke 22:31-32).

One of my all-time favorite cinematic scenes comes from the 1991 movie *City Slickers,* when the rough and hardened cowboy Curly (Jack Palance) and the greenhorn city slicker Mitch (Billy Crystal) ride along on their cattle drive, engaged in a deep existential conversation. Curly asks Mitch, "Do you know what the secret of life is?" Mitch replies, "No, what?" Curly holds up his index finger and, with the use of some colorful language, goes on to explain there's only one thing that matters in life. Mitch asks, "That's great, but what's the one thing?" To which Curly wisely responds, "That's what you gotta figure out."

For the Christian, what is our "one thing?" The most important attribute characterizing and permeating our life here on earth. Could our one thing, our answer to Curly's question, be the only thing Jesus prayed for when He prayed for Peter? Here, Jesus prayed only for Peter's *"faith."* That it would *"not fail."* And it didn't. Sure, he would soon deny Christ three times and need restoration from Jesus (John 21:15-19), but in the end, Peter's faith would not fail. In fact, Peter would boldly live the rest of his life filled with Christ and be full of faith, to the point where he would eventually articulate its worth and value, *"your faith, being much more precious than gold"* (1 Peter 1:7).

Our faith is our one thing. For without it, we cannot please God (Hebrews 11:6), nor can we manifest love. No faith? No Love. *Sola fide*: justification by faith alone. It's trusting Him, taking Him at His Word, and believing His promises. Not just knowing *about* them but having faith *in* them. Unlike the Israelites who wandered in the desert:

> *"For indeed the gospel was preached to us as well as to them; but the word which they heard did not profit them, not being mixed with faith in those who heard it"* (Hebrews 4:2).

We're called *believers* for a reason. So *"above all, take up your shield of faith"* (Ephesians 6:16), for we all want to hear, *"Well done, good and faithful* [faith full] *servant!"* (Matthew 25:23).

Step Out

*"Do not despise the day of small beginnings, for the Lord rejoices
to see the work begin" (Zechariah 4:10).*

There is such a thing as paralysis by analysis. Where overthinking a situation can cause forward motion to freeze, resulting in no course of action being taken at all. "What if this happens?" "But what about....?" To overcome this human and organizational tendency, a former employer of mine adopted a saying I came to be quite fond of: "50% today is better than 100% tomorrow." Because tomorrow never comes.

The Bible is full of this truth. In the verse above from Zechariah, we learn the principle of just starting. Sure, not everything will be buttoned up and pristine when you begin, but that's the point. In starting, you learn. And in learning, you grow in knowledge and understanding. This is the beauty of just doing it. *"Farmers who wait for perfect weather never plant. If they watch every cloud, they never harvest" (Ecclesiastes 11:4).* Farming conditions are never perfect when a farmer decides to plant or harvest.

When we start something without overthinking it, we are heeding Proverbs 3:5-6:

> *"Trust in the Lord with all your heart, and lean not on your own understanding; in all your ways acknowledge Him, and He shall direct your paths."*

Rather than leaning too much on our own understanding and explaining why we can't, starting with what God has laid on our hearts acknowledges our trust in Him and faith that, as we go, the Lord will direct our path. Consider the ten lepers who were healed (Luke 17:11-19). Jesus merely said, *"Go show yourselves to the priests."* In obedience, they started walking on their path......*before* they were healed. It was *"as they went"* when the healing occurred.

Or take Peter in a boat during a storm. While the other fearful eleven clung to the false security of the boat, Peter had the audacity to step out. Sure, he became afraid and began to sink, but Jesus was there. He's always there. So go ahead, step out. The Lord rejoices to see the work begin.

Is It Even Possible?

"Pray without ceasing" (1 Thessalonians 5:17).

If ever there was a verse that has stumped me over the years, it's the one quoted above. How in the world are we supposed to achieve that? At first blush, it seems to be an impossible assignment, given we have jobs to do, errands to run, conversations to engage in, emails to answer, children to raise, and a hundred logistical dilemmas to navigate each day. The mental model I picture when I imagine a life of ceaseless prayer is a monastic-like existence where grooves are made in the floor where knees daily reside. Sure, I pray, but *without ceasing*? How can we accomplish this, given our busy 21st-century lifestyles?

One encouraging connection I've recently made is the role of gratitude in this endeavor. When we are thankful, recognizing Him as the source of it all, prayer takes on an entirely different connotation. Gone is the need for a monastery. Consider the blessed water we Americans swim in. Both from a chronological (21st-century) and geographical (USA) perspective. Paved roads, microwaves, duct tape, coffee, heated homes, indoor plumbing, refrigeration, tires, sidewalks, flowers, mattresses, paper towels, rain, socks, deadbolts, cushioned chairs, and an invisible immune system constantly fighting to keep us healthy. Need I go on? This very short list is a microscopic drop in a tiny teacup scooped from the ocean of God's blessings in our lives. If we're mindful of all we have to be grateful to God for, suddenly, to pray without ceasing is doable as we go about our daily lives.

Take, for instance, the prayers found in the Bible. Study them, and you'll find gratitude the common denominator:

"Do not cease to give thanks" (Ephesians 1:16)
"Giving thanks to the Father" (Colossians 1:12)
"We give thanks to God always" (1 Thessalonians 1:2)

So, let's be grateful people. Begin giving thanks to Him for the big E stuff at the top of your life's eye chart, and your vision will soon improve. Before long, your gratitude eyesight will improve, and you'll realize you're giving thanks to Him throughout the day, and prayer will become as natural as breathing.

Lions, and Tigers, and Bears, Oh My!

"The news had come to the royal court of Judah: 'Syria is allied with Israel against us!' So the hearts of the king and his people trembled with fear, like trees shaking in a storm" (Isaiah 7:2).

The business of reporting the news is the business of making money. Higher ratings mean more money from advertisers. And fear sells. Thus the saying in the media industry is: *If it bleeds, it leads.* So, it shouldn't surprise us when we hear of intentional psychological agendas designed to prey on and heighten human anxieties. One simple ploy used by fear-based news possesses a twofold aim. First, to grab the viewer's attention via a teaser, and second, to persuade the viewer the solution will be found in the news story itself. For instance, if a teaser asks, "What's in your tap water that YOU need to know about? Story at 11," a viewer will likely tune in to get this most up-to-date information. Why? So they can be safe. Anxiety, fear, safety. In that order. Over and over and over again. Each and every unrelenting day.

Life in Isaiah's time was no different than ours. Sure, they didn't have television, social media, or the internet, but they did get the news. Reports about current events and what awful things may soon transpire were received then like they are today. Unfortunately, we just have access to so much more. Excruciatingly more. So, how can we digest and respond to this informational fire hose we drink from? How are we to protect ourselves from an industry designed to increase our anxiety and fear?

The solution is the same as the one which existed three thousand years ago. In response to the above news the royal court received, God said, *"Unless your faith is firm, I cannot make you stand firm"* (Isaiah 7:9). Faith and fear will never be friends. So, let's fixate the eyes of our hearts to the Lord and away from our devices. Let's look up and not down. In doing so, we will find the solid Rock upon which our hearts and minds can firmly stand:

> *"You will keep in perfect peace all who trust in You, all whose thoughts are fixed on You! Trust in the Lord always, for the Lord God is the eternal Rock"* (Isaiah 26:3-4).

Twenty Minutes to Live

"See then that you walk circumspectly, not as fools but as wise,
redeeming the time because the days are evil" (Ephesians 5:15-16).

On January 13, 2018, at 8:07 a.m. local time, an alert went out to all phones in Hawaii: BALLISTIC MISSILE THREAT INBOUND TO HAWAII. SEEK IMMEDIATE SHELTER. THIS IS NOT A DRILL. At a time when North Korean tensions were at a high, it would only take 20 minutes for one of their missiles to hit the island. And so, with a sense of complete terror and frantic urgency, a myriad of responses kicked in. Many parents removed manhole covers and stuffed their children into storm drains. Thousands contacted friends and family to express their love and say goodbye. Others opted to stay on the golf course because, as they said later, they might as well die doing something they loved. And, of course, many decided to livestream on social media in their last few minutes of life. Why miss a chance to go viral?

As you might surmise, it ended up being a false alarm. Authorities eventually posted a retraction 38 minutes later. But it does beg the question: What would you do if you only had 20 minutes to live?

In Greek, there are two words for the English word *time.* This first is *chronos,* which is the measurement of chronological time. Clocks, watches, and calendars. The second is *kairos.* Where chronos is quantitative, kairos is qualitative. It measures moments, not seconds. It refers to the right moment, the opportune moment, or a defining moment. Time judged not by duration, but by its importance and value. Time that is significant. And it is kairos which is used in the Ephesians passage above. We are to redeem the kairos.

So let's make the most of our special moments, those critical open doors in life and with other people. Those moments where significant deposits can be made into eternal investments. For you never know when your chronos will turn to kairos.

Vain Imaginations

"Because that, when they knew God, they glorified him not as God, neither were thankful, but became vain in their imaginations, and their foolish heart was darkened" (Romans 1:21).

According to the Oxford Dictionary, the word *vain* is defined as *Conceited: Having or showing excessive pride in one's appearance, abilities, or achievements.* When the Bible speaks of *"vain imaginations,"* it speaks to our thought life and the imaginary praise we seek and desire from our fellow humans.

Recently, I was mowing the lawn at our church. As I was listening to my music and minding my own business, suddenly, a brief thought flitted into my mind, imagining how impressed others would be with my mowing prowess. "Boy, I sure wish others mowed as well as Steve does." Oh, but it didn't stop there. A few days later, as I was setting up chairs at church, I imagined others praising me for the excellent, straight rows I had created. And lest we think a vain imagination is limited to grass and chairs, haven't we all imagined the praise we would receive about that new hairdo, my incredible children, our home décor, this cute outfit, my cool truck, the promotion at work, or my huge muscles? As John Calvin said, "The human heart is a factory of idols." *"Oh wretched man that I am! Who will deliver me from this body of death? I thank God – through Jesus Christ our Lord!"* (Romans 7:24-25).

To be able to imagine is a gift from God. With it, we create, seeing in our mind the possibilities for the future, enabling us to cast a vision for others. But when our imagination links up with our pride, guaranteed a vain imagination is just around the corner. Fortunately, the above passage from Romans 1 provides both the problem and the solution. The antidote for vanity is gratitude. Being a grateful person. When we give thanks to God and glorify Him, it protects our hearts from becoming foolish. We'll see Him as the source of every good and perfect gift, and for life itself. So please join me. The next time we experience a vain intrusion, let's take that thought captive, giving thanks….and glory….to God.

"Casting down imaginations, and every high thing that exalts itself against the knowledge of God, and bringing every thought to the obedience of Christ" (2 Corinthians 10:5).

Record Players

"It [love] does not dishonor others, it is not self-seeking, it is not easily angered, it keeps no record of wrongs" (1 Corinthians 13:5).

Long before there was Spotify and digital playlists, we prehistoric types had cassettes and albums. In fact, I can still remember the time my friend and I were in his car, and he showed me this new thing called CDs, where you could just hit a button and go right to the song of your choice. No way! Up until then, fast forward or rewind had been just a shot in the dark with cassettes. Unlike our beloved albums. Not only could you place the stylus of a record player precisely on the song of your choice, but you could activate the repeat feature and hear your favorite album over and over again. And while that was a prized feature back then, it's not so much in the repeated playing of life.

In our desire to love and *not* keep a record of wrongs, two warning signs should alert you to the presence of resentment and bitterness and the absence of forgiveness and healing. First, *bitterness remembers details*. Not the general memory of a person in our past but the detailed specificity of them and a particular event(s). "It was Tuesday, January 12th, 2006 at 8:15 am. She stormed into my office without knocking and, with her typical snide tone of voice, said…. " You can recall it verbatim. Like you were there. Why? Because you are. Over and over again, returning to the event, the person, the situation, repeating all the minute offenses again and again in your mind. Even discovering new ones as the album continues to repeat.

The second warning sign is the use of the words *always* and *never*. "You never do this." "You always do that." When we use these two tell-tale words, it's an indicator we've caught a repeat offender. The rap sheet of our mind has just logged another offense in a lengthy criminal record. The defendant has been found guilty and imprisoned, with no possibility of parole. Unless. Unless, by the grace of God, we, the judge and jury, wipe the slate clean. Like God did for us. In Christ. Only then can the album of the past stop spinning.

> *"For I will forgive their wickedness and will remember their sins no more"* (Hebrews 8:12).

Health Advice

"Trust in the Lord with all your heart, and lean not on your own understanding"
(Proverbs 3:5).

In our digital age, trying to self-diagnose our most recent ache or pain has become quite common. With just a few keystrokes, access to a plethora of medical information from around the world is at our fingertips. Some good, others not so much. For instance, for centuries it was believed "feed a cold and starve a fever" was true. Thinking colds came from cold temperatures, eating was recommended to fuel the body, while fevers, believed to be caused by hot temperatures, could be reduced by eliminating caloric intake. While this has been debunked, it does show misinformation is not reserved for our age alone.

While it may be false for our physical health, when it comes to our soul, this principle is, in fact, quite true. Especially when we find ourselves in a prolonged trial with the weight of the world placed upon our tiny shoulders. In times such as these, life's crushing load seems unbearable, and the tears flow frequently and freely. And with our only timestamp for deliverance being His promise *"in due time"* (1 Peter 5:6), we wonder when it will finally end.

This is the time to feed and starve. To feed our faith and starve our analysis. To look up to Him, when our natural proclivity is to obsessively look down on the problem at hand. For in a fiery trial, fear and anxiety activate an adrenaline rush, speeding up the analysis of our mind to fix our problem, come up with a solution, and escape ASAP the dark cloud hovering above us. And yet, this is the very propensity we need to starve. To *"Be still and know that I am God"* (Psalm 46:10), and to admit, *"we do not know what to do, but our eyes are upon You"* (2 Chronicles 20:12).

Here, then, is the fight of faith. To walk by faith and not by the sight of the trial. To feed your faith and the promises He's given in His Word instead. For in all my years, I have yet to meet a person in a trial who had too much Biblical faith and too little human analysis. Let us trust God, lean into Jesus, and by looking up to Him find the health our soul so desperately needs.

Inside Out

"Finally, brothers, whatever is true, whatever is honorable, whatever is right, whatever is pure, whatever is lovely, whatever is commendable, if there is any excellence and if anything worthy of praise, think about these things"
(Philippians 4:8).

Before coming to Jesus, I had a gutter mouth. Rarely could I speak a sentence without it laced with some sort of creative profanity. Soon after coming to Christ in college, I still clearly remember the two moments when the Holy Spirit would rid me of my expletive deletives.

The first instance was when we were playing a pick-up basketball game on the court at our fraternity. In the middle of the game, one of my dear "brothers" suddenly drove his truck onto the court for no apparent reason. I instinctually did what I had always done. I flipped him off. Immediately, I stared at my finger, shockingly aghast at what my trained hand had learned to habitually do. "Stop swearing and using these hand gestures," the inner voice spoke. How revolutionary this new voice and its directive were.

While I thought that surely sufficed, He was not through. Soon thereafter, I was walking back from classes, minding my own business. Suddenly, on the sidewalk right in front of the Tri Delt sorority, I heard the same voice whisper, "I want you to stop *thinking* of those words." Now I was shocked, realizing for the first time the Lord wanted not only my hands, feet, and mouth, but my mind also.

God wants to be Lord of your thought life. But how? The verse above provides us with the roadmap, for He knows our design. Like computers, garbage in, garbage out. Conversely, truth in, truth out. Lovely in, lovely out. Yes, God wants your body to be a living sacrifice, but where do you begin? You begin with your mind, for He knows your body will soon follow. *"Be transformed by the renewing of your mind, that you may prove what that good and acceptable and perfect will of God"* (Romans 12:2). That's where He begins, for mind renewal will birth transformation, and true transformation is always from the inside out.

Less is More

"So then, my beloved brethren, let every man be swift to hear, slow to speak, slow to wrath" (James 1:19).

The world loves a good speaker. Especially a good public speaker. Why do you think that is? One contributor might be, as studies have found, humanity's #1 fear is public speaking. #2 is death. In a bizarre and macabre sort of way, I guess the bulk of us would rather die than speak publicly! Given this strange reality, we tend to exalt those who do it well. Maybe a little more than we should.

On the other hand, listening doesn't seem to bubble up on any of the *What We Fear Most* surveys. Nor is it way up there on the coveted list of gifts, skills, and talents that will guarantee us a life of fame and fortune. And I've never seen the world's best listeners invited onto talk shows or have a popular podcast devoted to listening.

While most of us would rather die than speak publicly, that's typically not the case when conversing with another individual. We like to talk. A lot. And we like to talk especially about ourselves. What could possibly be more fascinating than me, myself, and I? Besides, it takes minimal effort because we know ourselves so very well. But knowing other people? Yeah, not so much. That would require listening. And that would be really hard. In fact, quite exhausting. Especially if we're called to truly listen to them. To the point of understanding. Like God does for us every day. Like Jesus did for us in becoming one of us. *"Don't look out only for your own interests, but take an interest in others, too" (Philippians 2:4).*

When it comes to conversing and developing close relationships, more is not more. Less is more. So let's develop those ears to hear, *"Anyone with ears to hear should listen and understand!"* (Matthew 11:15), strengthening our ear muscles while we give our vocal cords a much-needed rest. *"Those who control their tongue will have a long life; opening your mouth can ruin everything"* (Proverbs 13:3).

I Will Rise Again

"For though I fall, I will rise again. Though I sit in darkness, the Lord will be my light"
(Micah 7:8).

Years ago, I was looking for an inspirational quote I could place at the end of a presentation I was doing on resilience. Scrolling through Google Images, I landed on one that caught my eye:

"Adversity is just change that we haven't adapted
ourselves to yet." Aimee Mullins

That's a pithy quote. What a great way to end. Maybe she's a poet. Or author. Or some life coach or speaker. Like Coach Vince Lombardi and his famous quote, "It's not whether you get knocked down, it's whether you get up." Curious, I looked her up and discovered she was so much more than that. Born without fibula bones, she had both her legs amputated beneath the knee at the age of one. The prognosis? A wheelchair for the rest of her life. Which is why I was even more surprised by her accomplishments: Film and television actress, model, and NCAA D1 athlete. The subject of resilience was much more than a mere academic or inspirational pursuit for Aimee Mullins.

Bethany Hamilton's response to adversity took a similar path, albeit in entirely different circumstances. Surfing off the North Shore of Kauai at the age of thirteen, a 14-foot-long Tiger Shark attacked and severed her left arm to the shoulder. By the time she got to the nearest hospital, she had already lost over 60% of her blood. On the brink of death, she would recover and remarkably return to competitive surfing. She would later say:

"Bad things are bound to happen to everyone. That's life. Here's my advice: don't put all your hope and faith into something that could suddenly and easily disappear. And honestly, that's almost anything. The only thing that will never go away, that will never fail you, is God."

Adversity. If you are alive, it's in your life. *"Yet man is born to trouble as surely as sparks fly upward"* (Job 5:7). No one is immune. And yet, in the same breath, you too can bravely and resiliently declare,

"As for me, I look to the Lord for help. I wait confidently for God
to save me, and my God will certainly hear me" (Micah 7:7).

Psalm 91: At War

"He who dwells in the secret place of the Most High shall abide under the shadow of the Almighty. I will say of the Lord, 'He is my refuge and my fortress; my God, in Him I will trust'" (Psalm 91:1-2).

In WWI, a commander in the US Army's 91st Infantry Division gave each of his soldiers a card with the 91st Psalm printed on it. Captain Eddie Rickenbacker, the greatest fighter pilot of WW I, was on a tour of air bases in the Pacific Theater when he had to ditch his B-17. For the next 24 days, he and seven others floated in three small rubber rafts, reading from a small pocket Bible and memorizing Psalm 91 until the day of their rescue.

When the actor Jimmy Stewart enlisted in the US Army Air Corps during WW II, his father gave him a letter and enclosed Psalm 91. In May of 1940, many of the British soldiers trapped on the beaches of Dunkirk, France, had memorized Psalm 91 and shouted it out loud as the Luftwaffe planes strafed them from above.

Going to war, or experiencing any imminent life-and-death situation, has a way of focusing one's mind. Gone are the trivial pursuits of life and the petty irritants so apt to consume us in times of peace. Unfortunately, problems arise when a person at war believes they live in a time of peace. Such can be the state of the confused believer. Believing they exist in a time of peace, they live accordingly, not realizing the enemy of their soul is constantly on the spiritual offensive against them. So let's put on the full armor of God and fight accordingly, having Psalm 91 as our weapon as we go into our daily battle.

"For though we walk in the flesh, we do not war according to the flesh. For the weapons of our warfare are not carnal but mighty in God for pulling down strongholds" (2 Corinthians 10:3-4).

Psalm 91: Our Dwelling Place

"Because you have made the Lord, who is my refuge, even the Most High, your dwelling place, no evil shall befall you, for He shall give His angels charge over you, to keep you in all your ways" (Psalm 91:9-11).

What does it mean to make the Lord our *"dwelling place?"* As you read through Psalm 91, you'll see this referenced several times. And in the Psalm prior, Moses writes, *"Lord, You have been our dwelling place in all generations"* (Psalm 90:1). Two who participate in the *Flourish Through The Word* community have expressed it as follows:

"God has given me a sweet dwelling place when I am with Him. I feel like I have crawled into a cozy cave, I sit under His wings of love, and nothing from the outside world can touch me. The world spins around me in chaos and trouble, but when I'm in my place, the peace and comfort are indescribable. I am secure under the protection of my Heavenly Father and the God of the universe."

"We should not merely read the Word and pray but treat it as a time of intimacy with God. The more I seek the Lord out and draw near to Him, whether in tears or shouts of praise, the greater the feelings of intimacy. Everything is laid bare because there is no need to gain His love or approval. I can just rest. These feelings also increase my desire to protect the time I have. I forget where I am and forget myself when I'm praying. I am just talking to Him as one who has been forgiven much. I am grateful. I do find that I am in love with our Lord."

Love. Peace. Comfort. Security. Intimacy. Vulnerability. Forgiveness. Gratitude. This is our dwelling place, for our true home is His presence. *"Surely goodness and mercy shall follow me all the days of my life; and I will dwell in the house of the Lord forever"* (Psalm 23:6).

Psalm 91: His Authority is Yours

"You shall tread upon the lion and the cobra, the young lion and the serpent you shall trample underfoot" (Psalm 91:13).

Have you ever tread upon or trampled a lion or cobra? Me either. And yet, in another sense, we have. In Christ. For Christ defeated the roaring lion, *"Be sober, be vigilant; because your adversary the devil walks about like a roaring lion, seeking whom he may devour"* (1 Peter 5:8), and crushed the slithery serpent, *"So the great dragon was cast out, that serpent of old, called the Devil and Satan, who deceives the whole world"* (Revelation 12:9). In His death and resurrection, Christ subjected every spiritual principality and power under His dominion, for *"Jesus came and spoke to them, saying, All authority has been given to Me in heaven and on earth"* (Matthew 28:18). And that authority? He's delegated it to you.

Nowhere is this more evident than in Luke chapter ten. Here, Jesus sends out seventy of His followers to the cities and places He is about to go, deputizing them with power to heal the sick and to declare the kingdom of God (Luke 10:9). And upon coming back, what was their report? *"Lord, even the demons are subject to us in Your name"* (Luke 10:17). To which Jesus responded, *"Behold, I give you the authority to trample on serpents and scorpions, and over all the power of the enemy, and nothing shall by any means hurt you"* (Luke 10:19). And you are just like them. You have been deputized by Jesus.

You have been deputized with power and authority. His power and His authority. You are over your world, not under it. Why? Because of the victory of Christ on the cross, where He *"disarmed principalities and powers, He made a public spectacle of them, triumphing over them in it"* (Colossians 2:15). That victory is now yours in Jesus. Yes, *"In the world you will have tribulation; but be of good cheer, I have overcome the world"* (John 16:33). So let us go forward into the tribulation of daily life as a victor and not a victim. *"For everyone born of God overcomes the world"* (1 John 5:4).

"And the God of peace will crush Satan under your feet shortly. The grace of our Lord Jesus Christ be with you. Amen" (Romans 16:20).

Hebrews 11: But what about _____?

"...in prisons more frequently, in deaths often...five times I received forty stripes minus one, three times I was beaten with rods, once I was stoned; three times I was shipwrecked, in weariness and toil, in sleeplessness often, in cold and nakedness..."
(2 Corinthians 11:23-25, 27).

The promises of Psalm 91 are astounding. They speak of absolute victory and protection for believers who take refuge in God. But what about those times when we are afflicted, when severe sickness hits, when a surgery goes wrong, when the trial seems never-ending, or when someone we love dies? How does Psalm 91 relate to us in those times? For help, we need to venture over to Hebrews 11 to find our answer.

"Now faith is the substance of things hoped for, the evidence of things not seen" (Hebrews 11:1). True Bible faith is not blind optimism, a *hope so* wish, or an intellectual assent to doctrine. True Bible faith is a confident trust in, and obedience to, God and His Word despite circumstances and consequences. Simply put, God speaks, we hear, we trust, and then we act on it. *"Faith comes by hearing, and hearing by the word of God"* (Romans 10:17). The circumstances may be impossible, and the consequences frightening or unknown, but we obey His Word just the same and believe Him to do what is right and best.

Hebrews 11 speaks of those who subdued kingdoms, and those who were tortured. Those who stopped the mouths of lions, and those who were mocked and imprisoned. Those who received their dead raised to life, and those who were sawn in two. Their common, overcoming, victorious link? Their faith. Their trust. Their hope. No, one group wasn't victorious and the other defeated. ALL were victorious.

> *"If God is for us, who can be against us? He who did not spare His own Son, but delivered Him up for us all, how shall He not with Him also freely give us all things. Who shall separate us from the love of Christ? For I am persuaded that neither death nor life, nor angels nor principalities, nor things present nor things to come, shall be able to separate us from the love of God which is in Christ Jesus our Lord"* (Romans 8:31-32, 37, 39).

Are you persuaded?

His Job: To Speak

"It is written, 'Man shall not live by bread alone,
but by every word that proceeds from the mouth of God'" (Matthew 4:4).

To help with frequent confusion about life, my simplistic brain needs to create simple categories regarding my relationship with God. With so many voices out there (and in my mind), I really have to work to keep the incessant noise separated from the signal of God's voice. Specifically, what's His job, and what's mine? Nowhere is this clearer than when I compare Matthew chapter 8 with Matthew chapter 9.

"But only <u>speak a word</u> and my servant will be healed" (8:8). God's chosen job? To speak to us. And here's the good news: He already has. He spoke when He created the world, *"Then God said" (Genesis 1:3).* In fact, He gave us His very Word in the form of His Son, *"And the Word became flesh, and dwelt among us"* (John 1:14), and in these last days, God *"has spoken to us by His Son"* (Hebrews 1:2). All past tense. God fulfilled His end of the bargain (ok, the more appropriate term is *covenant*). And this is why Jesus said, *"It is finished"* (John 19:13). While God is still at work on the earth, His revelation is complete. God's Word and the finished work of Jesus Christ are whole and sufficient.

"And He cast out the spirits <u>with a word</u>, and healed all who were sick" (8:16). Just one word. That's all it took. For with God, less is more. *"For the word of God is living and powerful, and sharper than any two-edged sword"* (Hebrews 4:12).

"So the demons begged Him, saying, 'If you cast us out, permit us to go away into the heard of swine.' And He said to them, '<u>Go</u>'" (8:31-32). There it is. A specific example, where with just one word *"Go,"* the demons went.

Throughout Matthew chapter 8, we see a microcosm of the entire Bible: The supernatural power of the Word of God and His promises for us. His job? It's called the Bible. And His name is Jesus. The finished work of the Word made flesh, the finished work of Christ on the cross. And because of Jesus, *"all the promises of God in Him are Yes, and in Him Amen, to the glory of God"* (2 Corinthians 1:20).

God has spoken.

Our Job: To Believe

"Jesus answered and said to them, 'This is the work of God,
that you believe in Him whom He sent.'" (John 6:29).

So God has spoken, and He's faithful to keep His Word. He's trustworthy, which simply means He is worthy of our trust. Unlike fallen and frail humans, His Word is His bond. And all of this is laid out for us in Matthew chapter 8. But what about us? What's our job? For that, we turn to Matthew chapter 9.

"When Jesus saw their faith, He said to the paralytic, 'Son, be of good cheer; your sins are forgiven you'" (9:2). Here's a great example of why having godly friends is essential! Bottom line, our job is to take Him at His Word. God places a huge premium on our faith. If you have any doubt, please read Hebrews chapter 11.

"Be of good cheer, daughter; your faith has made you well" (9:22). Twelve years she had been bleeding. But she believed that a touch of Christ's hem would heal her. And it did.

"According to your faith, let it be to you" (9:29). Two blind men sought the mercy of Jesus. And they got it. The blind now saw.

Faith. Trust. Belief. That's our job. He did all the work, so now we just need to believe it. One brief point and then a story. This isn't about getting worked up into a faith tizzy. "The problem is that you don't have enough faith!!" That puts all the emphasis on you. As though it's all up to you. No, this is all about the *object* of your faith. I could have incredible faith in a paper mâché chair, but that chair will not support me despite my great faith. Conversely, I could have minuscule faith that a solid wood chair will hold me up, but regardless, when I timidly sit down, I'll be just fine. Why? Because my object was faithful. Now, over time, as I keep experiencing how faithful these wooden chairs are, my faith in them will grow. That's just natural. And so it is with God.

Now for the story. I once heard of a man who had cancer. Throughout his journey, he believed God would heal him. On his deathbed, as his pastor stood by, his last words to him were, "Pastor, I'm still believing." What a beautiful testimony of someone doing their job to the very end. In this case, God chose to heal him in heaven. For others, He chooses to do so on earth. But our job? Our job is to believe Him. Regardless of what we see, feel, or experience.

So, let's stay focused on our job and let God do His.

Bible Bravery
Our Examples

"Follow my example, as I follow the example of Christ"
(1 Corinthians 11:1).

"Faithless is he that says farewell when the road darkens."
J.R.R. Tolkien

Our Examples

Growing up, my hero was Willie Mays. Willie was one of the greatest baseball players who ever lived. Inducted into the Hall of Fame in 1979 in his first year of eligibility, I've lost count of the number of times I've gazed at the picture or watched the video of "The Catch," the time he caught the long drive off the bat of Vic Wertz in the 1954 World Series. In fact, I can, to this day, show you the exact place where Mom and I were in the car when I opened my Topps baseball card pack and beheld the Holy Grail of baseball cards. What a magical moment in a young boy's life, forever etched as a core memory of innocent joy.

Now that I'm older and battle-hardened by the realities of life, I still need heroes today. Maybe not so much of the sports-star variety, but heroes, nonetheless. Ones that point me to God as I near the finish line of life, now having more years behind me than those that lie ahead. And while I can only read about and imagine what it must feel like to run a marathon (the last 5k I "ran" many years ago was entirely walked), I do have some experience running the marathon of life. Thus far, I can attest it requires, by grace, much patience, endurance, and perseverance. And nearing the end of said race, my experience tells me temptation and weariness will continue to lurk just below the surface, calling me to quit. There they will remain to the very end, nipping at my heels in the hope I, too, will trip and fall before I finish, just as King Solomon did so long ago.

This is where the heroes of the faith come in—those who ran to the end and finished well. Abraham, Hagar, Sarah, David, Daniel, and Paul, to name just a few. Not perfect, but honest, authentic, vulnerable men and women whom God loved, and they loved in return. We can learn so much from them and their lives, drawn to their combined human frailty and love for God. So let's study those who finished well. Who knows. In doing so, we may discover a hero who will forever etch in our souls a faith to finish strong, too.

"Do you not know that those who run in a race, all run, but one receives the prize? Run in such a way that you may obtain it"
(1 Corinthians 9:24).

Hagar: I See You

"She gave this name to the Lord who spoke to her: 'You are the God who sees me,' for she said, 'I have now seen the One who sees me'" (Genesis 16:13).

If you were asked to provide an example of courage, I doubt it would be about someone in full-blown retreat. Instead, you would probably describe a person or persons who moved forward in the face of danger. Like a person charging into a burning house to save those in it, or the Allied forces storming the beaches of Normandy. To remember and to inspire, these are the stories of heroism we write books and produce movies about. But I wonder if the far more frequent acts of bravery are counterintuitively mundane and simple—the daily run-of-the-mill kind. Like when life has run you over, everything within you wants to quit, and getting out of bed in the morning requires every ounce of strength you can muster. If you can relate, meet Hagar the Brave.

The story is told in Genesis 16. Despite trying for over a decade, Abram and Sarai cannot have a child. Although foreign to us, in that culture, it was acceptable to continue one's lineage through the wife's maidservant. So, at Sarai's insistence, Hagar becomes pregnant by Abram, and they live happily ever after. Well, not quite. When Sarai learns Hagar has conceived, Hagar *"became despised in her eyes"* (v 4). Sarai then *"dealt harshly with her,"* so *"she fled from her presence"* (v 6). Kicked out, the despised Hagar was homeless and pregnant through no fault of her own. What would she do? Where would she go? Abandoned and forsaken, she was all alone.

Or was she? The Angel of the Lord found her (v 7), restored her, and gave her the courage to return and move forward in life. And the source of her newfound strength? Hagar realized she was seen. She was known. By name. The Lord was with her and saw her when no one else did. *"Then she called the name of the Lord who spoke to her, You-Are-the-God-Who Sees" (v 13).*

Like Hagar, maybe you are on the retreat. Feeling alone and invisible, feelings of abandonment have become your constant companion. But you have another One with you. *"Lahai Roi"* (v 14)...the God who sees....sees you. He knows intimately what you are going through, and by His grace, you've shown great courage this morning by merely getting up and facing the difficult day ahead. While no book will be written or movie made on what happened today, the Author of your faith sees and records it all. And that act of courage He will never forget.

Abraham: What's Your Name?

"No longer shall your name be called Abram, but your name shall be called Abraham; for I have made you a father of many nations" (Genesis 17:5).

Please note. *"I have made you a father of many nations."* Past tense. Which logically doesn't make any sense. Abram and Sarai aren't parents. Sure, he's a father of Ishmael via Hagar (Genesis 16:1-4), but God promised a son for Abram and his wife Sarai. But they've been trying to have a child for 25 long years! Nothing. Isn't it obvious? They're infertile. And God is now saying this 100-year-old man and 90-year-old woman will conceive? And on top of that, He wants to rename them? Abram is going to go by Abraham, the father of many nations. And Sarai will go by Sarah, the princess of a multitude, *"... a mother of nations"* (Genesis 17:16). And all of this *before* a pregnancy? This is weird. At least for us humans. But not for Him.

Seeing the end from the beginning, God was calling them what they would become. That's what He does. And what He did for them, He does for us. And our response? Like Abram, it's simply to believe. To take God at His Word. *Before* we can see with our eyes. That's called faith. *"And he [Abram] believed in the Lord, and He accounted it to him for righteousness"* (Genesis 15:6).

Maybe you're not feeling fearless today. Perhaps you're feeling weak and insignificant, and want to hide and run away from it all. No matter. What God says about you in His Word is the truth about who you really are. Regardless of your past. Independent of what others have said about you. Separate from how you see and perceive yourself. For, in the end, you are who He says you are. Like Gideon. Hiding in a winepress in fear of the Midianites, an angel of the Lord appears and calls him who he is, a *"mighty warrior"* (Judges 6:12), before he ever was.

As Roy Hicks said,

> "Let God's words, which designated His will and promise for your life, become as fixed in your mind and as governing of your speech as God's changing Abraham's name was in shaping his concept of himself. Do not 'name' yourself anything less than God does."

Sarah: No Laughing Matter

"Therefore Sarah laughed within herself, saying, 'After I have grown old, shall I have pleasure, my lord being old also?'" (Genesis 18:12).

Laughter is a gift from God. With so much adversity and pain, we feeble humans always need to keep an ample supply of laughter handy in the medicine cabinet of life. Without a daily dose, we're bound to catch the contagious illnesses of gloom, despair, and negativity. As I frequently said throughout my career as we faced daily pressure, dysfunction, and stress, "There's a very fine line between laughing and crying. I choose to laugh."

And yet, the Bible says there's *"A time to weep, and a time to laugh"* (Ecclesiastes 3:4). While laughter at the right time is therapy for the soul, laughter at the wrong time is, let's say, awkward. Which brings us to Sarah in Genesis chapter 18. For 25 years, Abraham and Sarah have been trying to have a baby. And for 25 years, nothing. Three hundred times (25 years x 12 months/year), Sarah got her monthly reminder she was barren. Then the Lord comes to them in Genesis 18 and says, this time next year, you'll have your baby. And 90-year-old Sarah laughed. To paraphrase, "Are you kidding me? My biological clock stopped ticking years ago." Insert awkward moment here.

The Lord's response to her unbelief? *"Is anything too hard for the Lord? At the appointed time I will return to you, according to the time of life, and Sarah shall have a son"* (Genesis 18:14). Two important "A" words there: *Anything* and *appointed*. For this was the same Sarah who, 13 years earlier, had decided SHE would appoint the time. Leaning on her own understanding, she neglected to wait for the Lord to bring what He had promised to fruition.

What about you? Are you tempted to laugh at the promises of God and think, "There's no way." Truth be told, I think there's a little bit of Sarah in all of us. And so the Lord's question to Sarah is His question to us today: Is anything too hard for Me? Run your circumstances through the filter of God's promises, and you'll get the same answer every time. An emphatic "No!" Bravery is the by-product of belief, so let's declare:

My finances are not too hard for God!
My marriage strain is not too hard for God!
My unemployment is not too hard for God!
My sickness is not too hard for God!

What's on your impossible list for today?

Sarah: His Name is Laughter

*"And Sarah said, 'God has made me laugh, and all who hear will laugh with me'"
(Genesis 21:6).*

Sure enough, at the appointed time, Sarah gave birth to their son Isaac, whose name means "laughter" in Hebrew. The 25-year trial was over. God had visited Abraham and Sarah in their impossible situation. What He had promised, He had fulfilled—in His way and on His timetable. No longer were they stuck in the cynical laughter of unbelief but were now filled with a laughter of joy and gratitude to God, with whom all things are possible.

So again, what's on your list of impossibles and unsolvables? Learning from Sarah, may we not take matters – or their timing – into our own hands. Instead, may God grant us the faith to believe and wait for Him. To that end, a friend recently sent us the following text:

> "I started asking myself – in the past, have I mocked or laughed to myself at His promises, walking in unbelief? I have seen Him as Lord, but have I seen Him as LORD? Have I believed He loves me enough for my impossible? For some of them but not for others?
>
> 'Yes, Lord, your Word says nothing is too hard for You.' The Bible confirms this over and over again – I can do all things through Christ. I am now responding and praying back to Him, 'Nothing is too hard for the Lord!'"

You can also escape if you feel stuck in the vortex of unbelief. Today, right now, you too can say about your impossibles, "Nothing is too hard for the Lord!" *"Oh, magnify the Lord with me, and let us exalt His name together"* (Psalm 34:3). Like Sarah, let's go from doubt to faith. Let's take God at His Word and trust Him, believing He is able. And in doing so, we too, like Sarah, will be commended by Him for that very same faith:

> *"By faith Sarah herself also received strength to conceive seed, and she bore a child when she was past the age, because she judged Him faithful who had promised"* (Hebrews 11:11).

Abraham: Take Now Your Son

"Then He said, 'Take now your son, your only son Isaac, whom you love, and go to the land of Moriah, and offer him there as a burnt offering on one of the mountains of which I shall tell you'" (Genesis 22:3).

Isaac, the child of promise. The beloved, only child of Abraham and Sarah. Born to Abraham, *"who did not waver at the promise of God through unbelief, but was instead strengthened in faith, giving glory to God"* (Romans 4:20). For 25 long years, he had waited and trusted God for the child He had promised. Now, Abraham was the grateful recipient of that gift from God. For many years, he enjoyed a loving father-son relationship, up to and including the day when God would speak to him once again about his beloved son.

"Offer him there as a burnt offering." "Wait, what? You now want me to sacrifice....kill...my promised son?" This would now be the ultimate test of Abraham's faith: Would the Lord's provision be strategically located along the pathway of his faithful obedience? For Abraham, the answer was an emphatic "YES!" There was no hesitation, *"So Abraham rose early in the morning"* (v. 3), and there was no doubt, *"My son, God will provide for Himself the lamb for a burnt offering"* (v. 8).

For Abraham, if God said it, then it was settled. He didn't take a few days to think and pray about it. He didn't spend time fasting or laying out fleeces to see if he really did hear from God. He didn't go around texting a ton of friends, asking them, "What would you do if you were me?" While true for the gray matters of life, *"in a multitude of counselors there is wisdom"* (Proverbs 11:14), this was not one of those situations. For Abraham, delayed obedience would have been clear disobedience. The unmistakable Word of God was enough for him.

This is what the brave do. When God has clearly spoken in His Word, knowing God can be trusted, they go. They move forward. So, like Abraham, we also need not fear when God's direction might be difficult for us to understand. Why is that? Because God can be trusted on the other side of our obedience. Is there a clear word God has given you in the Bible? Then go. He will be there on the other side waiting for you.

Abraham: The Lord Will Provide

"And Abraham called the name of the place, The-Lord-Will-Provide; as it is said to this day, 'In the Mount of the Lord it shall be provided'" (Genesis 22:14).

It's much easier to say, "The Lord did provide," than "The Lord will provide." Hindsight is always 20/20. But here's a father, taking his only promised son on a three-day journey to the land of Moriah. Why? To sacrifice him, as the Lord had instructed him to do. But ahead of time, he believed *"God was able to raise him up"* (Hebrews 11:19) and that *"God will provide for Himself the lamb"* (v. 8). Whether by resurrection or a substitutionary lamb, one way or another, Abraham knew in advance he was coming off that mountain with his son, to where he could say to his servants, *"and we will come back to you"* (v. 5). He *will* provide. And we *will* be coming back.

And yet, after the fact, he names the place not "The Lord Did Provide," but "The Lord Will Provide. Why is that? Because just like Isaac, in this exact same land of Moriah, Jesus some 2,000 years later, the only begotten son of His Father, the promised Messiah, would be sacrificed, buried for three days, and then rise again. Abraham was looking forward, in faith, to his Savior, the Lord Jesus Christ, because he knew the Lord would provide. He always does.

Like Abraham, we too can confidently say The Lord Will Provide. For our finances. Our health. Our churches. Our relationships. Our children. For it all.

> *Though troubles assail us, and dangers affright*
> *Though friends should all fail us, and foes all unite.*
> *Yet one thing secures us, whatever betide:*
> *The Scripture assures us, "The Lord will provide."*
>
> *The birds, without barn or storehouses are fed;*
> *From them let us learn to trust God for our bread;*
> *His saints what is fitting shall ne'er be denied,*
> *So long as 'tis written, "The Lord will provide."*
>
> *When Satan appears to stop up our path,*
> *And fills us with fears, we triumph by faith;*
> *He cannot take from us, though oft he has tried,*
> *The heart-cheering promise, "The Lord will provide."*
>
> *When life sinks apace, and death is in view,*
> *The word of His grace shall comfort us through;*
> *Not fearing or doubting, with Christ on our side,*
> *We hope to die shouting, "The Lord will provide."*

Moses: Send Someone Else

"Then Moses said to the Lord, 'O Lord, I am not eloquent, neither before nor since You have spoken to Your servant; but I am slow of speech and slow of tongue. Send someone else'" (Exodus 4:10, 13).

We all have inadequacies, shortcomings, and insecurities. Gaps between what is and what we think it should be. *It* could be our intelligence, income, athleticism, weight, beauty, material possessions, prayer life, public speaking ability, generosity, social skills, time management, love for God, love for others, etc. Need I go on? Basically, everything. We humans fall short and must plead *guilty as charged* across the spectrum of life.

Brene Brown, in her book *Daring Greatly*, calls this way of thinking "scarcity" and describes it as follows:

> "A mindset where individuals feel like they are 'never enough,' constantly lacking something whether it be success, validation, or even just enough time, leading to a sense of shame through constant comparison to others and a fear of not measuring up."

And a mindset of "I can't…" will ultimately lead to the conclusion of "…therefore, I won't."

Moses had this mindset. "Send someone else, Lord, I'm not the guy." Moses felt disqualified because of His limitation. But maybe the very thing we believe limits us is the very thing that qualifies us. In our counterintuitive Christian life, why is it that Paul says, *"When I am weak, then I am strong" (2 Cor. 12:10)*? That's crazy talk….unless you are in Christ. For in Christ, our very weakness actually empowers and qualifies us, *"He [Christ] said to me [Paul], 'My grace is sufficient for you, for My strength is made perfect in weakness'" (2 Cor. 12:9)*. The cross of Christ was the great exchange, for there, God gives us His strength in exchange for our weakness.

So don't look at your inadequacies and insufficiencies. Look away. Look to Jesus. He is your adequacy. He is your sufficiency. So now, like Isaiah, you can say, *"Here am I! Send me" (Isaiah 6:8)*.

Joshua: Arise and Go

"Moses my servant is dead. Now therefore, arise, go over this Jordan, you and all the people, to the land which I am giving them – the children of Israel" (Joshua 1:2).

In His final words before He ascended into heaven, Jesus said to His disciples, *"Go therefore and make disciples of all the nations...."* (Matthew 28:19). Called *The Great Commission*, His directive to them is His directive to us also. Every person's "go" will be a unique assignment designed beautifully by Him for you, but our common denominator is we all can learn from Joshua how to do so successfully.

Linger in the presence of God *("Joshua the son of Nun, a young man, did not depart from the tabernacle" Exodus 33:11)* – You will go through many seasons in life. Some busy, others not so much. Regardless, pray for and seek a hunger to be in His presence. In some seasons, the time might be short and at other times longer, but pray that His presence would be the magnetic pull of your life. Like it was for Joshua.

Believe beforehand in the victory *("Every place that the sole of your foot will tread upon I have given you" Joshua 1:3)* – Every promise is yes and amen in Christ Jesus our Lord. While every promise in the Bible has direct application to the context in which it was written, it also is true God has taken all of those promises and given them to you. So, everywhere you set your feet, God has given it to you. In Christ, you win because He won. Believe it!

He is always with you *("As I was with Moses, so I will be with you. I will not leave you nor forsake you" Joshua 1:5)* – When God gave Joshua his big assignment (go into Canaan), His presence was His promise. When Jesus gave His disciples their big assignment (go into the world), His one promise was once again his presence, *"I am with you always, even to the end of the age"* (Matthew 28:20). His presence is your confidence and boldness in going forward.

Read and meditate on the Bible *("This Book of the Law shall not depart from your mouth, but you shall meditate in it day and night" Joshua 1:8)* – Jesus said people can't live on just food alone, but on every Word that proceeds from the mouth of God. If you have an assignment as big as Joshua's, *and you do*, then you need God's Word just as much as he did.

Be strong and courageous *("Be strong and of good courage; do not be afraid, nor be dismayed" Joshua 1:9)* – Fear, worry, anxiety, alarm, etc. These are all part of the human dilemma. God knows this. But He says that's okay, because I'm always with you. And because of that, you can say with courage, "I've got this" because He has you.

Gideon: Name Calling

"When the angel of the Lord appeared to Gideon, he said,
'The Lord is with you, mighty warrior'" (Judges 6:12).

Marjie and I recently enjoyed a whale-watching adventure with our two-year-old granddaughter, Indie. Granted a lollipop at the beginning of the voyage, about halfway through, we observed more lollipop on her (and others!) than could have possibly been in her. At which time I remarked, "Indie, are you a sticky girl?" To which she corrected me by replying, "No, I'm Indie girl."

Suffice it to say Indie is off to a great start in life. She knows who she is. Despite the name-calling from her grandfather (AKA G-Daddy), she stood her ground and proclaimed who she really was. What an important life lesson, for in this life, no one will be immune from the barrage of name-calling we will receive. In the home, on the playground, at school, or in the workplace, every believer will hear words challenging and questioning their true identity in Christ. Names such as fat, lazy, dumb, slow, bimbo, four-eyes, weak, or dork just scratch the surface. To counteract this assault from the outside, like Indie, we must stay anchored to the One who calls us each by name.

Before timid Gideon would be used by God to deliver Israel, while he was in hiding for fear of the Midianites, God called him a *"mighty warrior."* Before ninety-year-old Sarah would conceive, God renamed her husband Abram, *"... your name shall be Abraham; for I have made you a father of many nations"* (Genesis 17:5). And today, whatever names you may have been called in the past, God calls you to Himself, by name. *"Do not fear, for I have redeemed you; I have called you by name; you are mine"* (Isaiah 43:1).

God knows the redeemed by name. Yes, your specific name. And He sees what He has planted in you, even though you may be currently unaware. Loved and accepted in Christ, the Lord has a plan, a hope, and a future for you. So let's learn from Indie and Gideon, for the name the Lord calls us is the only one that matters.

David and Goliath

"David said, 'The Lord, who delivered me from the paw of the lion and from the paw of the bear, He will deliver me from the hand of this Philistine'" (1 Samuel 17:37).

Most of us are familiar with the story of David and Goliath. If not, I encourage you to read 1 Samuel 17. In a nutshell, Israel was once again fighting their arch-nemesis, the Philistines. But in this battle, the Philistines had an ace in the hole: a giant named Goliath—all 9 feet 9 inches of him. For 40 days, he would come out and taunt the chickens of Israel, challenging them to send a man he could fight in a winner-take-all battle. Then along comes this shepherd boy, sent by his father to bring refreshments to his brothers, and soon, everything would change.

To paraphrase, David's initial reaction goes something like this, "Who does this guy think he is, coming against the armies of the Living God?" He goes to King Saul and says, "Let me at him!"

Where did David come up with such bravery? It wasn't his self-confidence. It came from God's faithfulness in his past (v. 37). Let's not miss what is happening here! While King Saul and his army focused on the sight and sound of Goliath, David focused on the goodness of God *instead*. David was not listening to the taunts, lies, and insults of the enemy but, by faith, remained preoccupied with God. David was too busy being fascinated by Him and who He is that he didn't fall for the intimidation tactics of his enemy.

David was a man after God's own heart. In all those long days and nights spent in the pasture with the sheep, his thoughts would default to God and the worship of Him. His empowerment to face the giant head-on was because David was trusting Him. The Lord was more real to David than Goliath was. Refusing to fear, David's attention was elsewhere. He was looking up while everyone else was looking down.

As was David, you have been empowered. You, like David, can look in the rearview mirror of your life and see His faithfulness. His provision. Yes, the enemy will attempt to sow seeds of fear, offense, insults, and insecurities in you, but you possess the power to be brave in Christ. Instead.

David: Great and Precious

"His divine power has given to us all things that pertain to life and godliness...
have been given to us exceedingly great and precious promises...
that through these you may be partakers of the divine nature" (2 Peter 1:3-4).

If you are honest with yourself, what comes to mind when you ponder your future? What do you expect to receive....or lose? Do you have dismal forebodings or fears? Maybe all you can see are large and intimidating enemies right before you. Ones that taunt, offend, accuse, and malign you. Much like David's reality, when a simple errand to the Valley of Elah turned into something far greater.

While you may be up against a few giants of your own, like David, you can carry the expectation of victory, for you are also an overcomer (1 John 5:4). Why? Because Jesus overcame (John 16:33).

Despite what you may be seeing or hearing, God intends the opposite to occur in your life. When you are on the receiving end of taunts, offenses, and accusations, the Lord has an *instead* for you. Beauty for ashes. Strength for weakness. Life for death. Carrying the expectation of the goodness of God wherever you go, be overcome by Him and His goodness. Determine not to be used by your circumstances, but use your circumstances to find that *instead* He promised you in Scripture. For your circumstances don't define His goodness; instead, His goodness defines your circumstances.

In receiving, by faith, the great and precious promises found in the Bible, we, too, can be brave. To count on God. Instead. This is why we are told in Scripture to *"renew our minds"* according to His Word. So let us take God at His Word, *"looking unto Jesus, the author and finisher of our faith"* (Hebrews 12:2).

> *"To all who mourn in Israel, He will give a crown of beauty for ashes, a joyous blessing instead of mourning, festive praise instead of despair. Instead of shame and dishonor, you will enjoy a double share of honor" (Isaiah 61:3, 7).*

David: The Signal

"David then led his men to Jerusalem to fight against the Jebusites...
The Jebusites taunted David, saying, 'You'll never get in here!
Even the blind and lame could keep you out!'" (2 Samuel 5:6).

David seemed to always be on the receiving end of taunting and mocking. His enemies took great delight in hurling insults his way. Here, we read about the Jebusites, and before we read about Goliath, *"Am I a dog, that you come to me with sticks?"* (1 Samuel 17:43). But it wasn't only his enemies who loved to abuse David verbally. Even his band of brothers came against him. In fact, they wanted to take their words to another level. To a physical one. After the Amalekites had captured all their loved ones, we read, *"David was greatly distressed, for the people spoke of stoning him"* (1 Samuel 30:6). Friend or foe, it seems as though everyone had it out for the one who sought after God's own heart.

Like David, we all have two types of sounds streaming into our lives. There's the cacophony of shrill *noise* our world serves up 24/7, and then there's the gentle cadence of His still, small voice found in His Holy Word—our *signal*. And while David never had to deal with social media or a 24/7 news feed, like us, he did have to choose: Which voice will I make the loudest in my life? Which voice will I truly listen to?

David went on to capture Jerusalem from the Jebusites, kill Goliath, and be reunited with his loved ones after defeating the Amalekites. He listened to the signal and thus possessed the courage needed to perform these (and many other) feats. You are no different from David. In receiving Christ, you received His power and the ability to overcome. In Christ, you are a victor, not a victim. So, like David, let's listen to the signal of God's goodness and greatness in our daily worship of Him. And be brave.

"I will bless the Lord at all times; His praise shall continually be
in my mouth. Oh, magnify the Lord with me, and let us exalt His
name together" (Psalm 34:1, 3).

Jehoshaphat: Fixated

"And Jehoshaphat feared, and set himself to the seek the Lord....we do not know what to do, but our eyes are on You" (2 Chronicles 20:12).

I have never been a gymnast, nor have I ever been on a balance beam. Watching the Olympics is probably the closest I'll ever come. At my age, not losing my balance while standing is a victory. So I found it interesting when I came across the following on how to stay on a balance beam when performing various flips and spins:

> In gymnastics, especially on the beam, the role of a focused gaze, commonly referred to as "spotting," is crucial for achieving precise and stable performances. A focused gaze helps gymnasts maintain spatial orientation while performing different skills on the beam. By fixing their eyes on a specific point, usually at the end of the beam, gymnasts can improve their balance and execute movements with increased precision. The gymnast selects a static point along the beam's axis and keeps their gaze locked on this point. This visual fixation serves as a visual anchor, reducing distractions and helping to align the body's movements with the beam.

A focused gaze. A visual fixation. All in an effort to reduce disorientation and remain on that narrow beam.

Life is like a balance beam. As we flip and spin, how quickly we can become disoriented. Just ask Jehoshaphat. With an allied army coming his way to slaughter his people, the King was outnumbered and overwhelmed. What's a king to do? Of course he was scared. But Jehoshaphat did something. He fixed his eyes on his never-changing God. The Immutable One. He who *"is the same yesterday, today, and forever"* (Hebrews 13:8). While Jehoshaphat didn't know what to do, his eyes were on the One who did.

Like Peter, with our eyes on Jesus, we too can walk on water. But take our eyes off Him? Start gazing at the wind and waves of life? Be assured sinking is in your not-too-distant future. So, as you go about the many flips and spins of life, daily recalibrate your visual fixation on Him who never moves, your visual anchor in the storm.

Jesus, we don't know what to do, but our eyes are on you.

Daniel: Courage in the Little Things

"But Daniel purposed in his heart that he would not defile himself with the portion of the king's delicacies, nor with the wine which he drank" (Daniel 1:8).

What images or stories come to mind when you think of the courageous? Do you think of Christian martyrs, such as those burned so Nero's evening garden parties might have lighting? Or those beheaded by ISIS for their faith? Maybe it's the heroic GI who fell on a grenade to save his platoon? Or perhaps the video of a parent standing up at a school board meeting to express her moral convictions? These and so many more are the brave, those who, in the face of hostile opposition, sacrificially stood alone with no regard for personal cost. Books are written and movies are made about such heroes. But where did they start? What did that first brave baby step look like?

In the book of Daniel, we have some of the most well-known and beloved stories of Biblical bravery. A fiery furnace, a hand writing on the wall, and a den of lions make for great Sunday school lessons. But one lesser-known story in Daniel typically does not make the cut. In chapter one, there's the story of the teenager Daniel and his three friends, captured by the Babylonians, 900 miles from home, and enslaved in a three-year training program. No human rights commission to appeal to, no friendly government to intervene, and no dream team of lawyers to represent them. They were under a king accountable to no one. God was all they had.

But right at the beginning, Daniel drew a line. He knew eating food offered to idols was an indirect way of giving tribute to them. How easy it would have been for him to think, "Well, Lord, you know in my heart, I'm not giving tribute to those idols, and a guy does need to eat." But he didn't, and as a result, verse nine says, *"Now God had brought Daniel into the favor and goodwill of the chief of the eunuchs."* The brave application? Favor and goodwill might just be on the other side of your honor of, and obedience to, the Lord in the "little" things.

Of course, as we'll soon see, obedience and honor of God must always be independent of the potential consequences of those actions. Whether they be good or bad for you personally. For regardless, He is always on the other side. And that is always good. So do not be afraid to stand alone because, in reality, you never are.

Daniel: Danger Zone

"So the decree went out, and they began killing the wise men;
and they sought Daniel and his companions, to kill them.
Then with counsel and wisdom Daniel answered" (Daniel 2:13-14).

Soon after Daniel and his friends made that initial death-defying choice not to eat the king's food, that same king had a disturbing dream (Daniel 2:1-3). Trouble was he wouldn't tell anyone what it entailed. He wanted someone to tell him both the dream and the interpretation. That's a tough one! In fact, all of his astonished court counselors and wise men said it was impossible. Well, that just made matters worse. The enraged king threw a hissy fit and commanded all these wise men to be killed and cut into pieces. What a guy! Enter Daniel, stage right.

The military commander came to arrest Daniel and carry out the execution. With death staring him in the face, Daniel didn't run or try and escape. He did *not* lean on his own understanding. Instead, he respectfully asked why and asked for an audience with the king. With everyone's life hanging in the balance and the clock ticking, Daniel asked his three friends to pray for him, putting his faith in the Living God alone. So to his prayer closet he went. And there, Daniel received not only the dream, but the interpretation. His response? All glory to God!

"Blessed be the name of God forever and ever, for wisdom and might are His. And He changes the times and the seasons; He removes kings and raises up kings; He gives wisdom to the wise and knowledge to those who have understanding. I thank You and praise You O God of my fathers" (Daniel 2:20-23).

Sometimes, we are called upon to do hard things in situations we had no time to prepare for – like facing sudden execution – but real growth almost always takes place when God puts us outside of our comfort zone. When events and circumstances far outside of our control come crashing down upon us and force us to respond. Prepare now, for no house built on a rock was ever constructed while the rain, floods, and winds raged. It's always before.

Daniel: Jesus is in The Fire

"'Look!'" he answered, 'I see four men loose, walking in the midst of the fire; and they are not hurt, and the form of the fourth is like the Son of God.'" (Daniel 3:25).

It's hard to pinpoint just how many Jews were taken 900 miles from Judah to Babylon once the deportations began in 586 B.C. Estimates range anywhere from 7,000 to 20,000 Jews. So it's probably safe to say when King Nebuchadnezzar got the idea to set up a 90-foot-tall golden image (Daniel 3:1-7), many Jews were in attendance. It's also probably safe to say that when the music started playing, everyone bowed down and worshiped the image, including all the Jews in attendance. All that is, except three: Shadrach, Meshach, and Abed-Nego.

Having stood alone regarding their diet, and after seeing their prayers answered just hours before execution, Daniel's three amigos were ready for action. They had seen God act in power, and now their faith was ready for a graduate-level course in bravery. And they would not be disappointed! Taken out to the plain of Dura, there it was. Ninety feet of gold towering over the gathered assembly. The threat of the fiery furnace was made, the band kicked in, and the three just stood there. You can imagine what happened next. After his minions made him aware, the emotive King Neby flew into a rage and cranked that furnace up even more. Death to the infidels! But it didn't phase them. To paraphrase, they replied, "Go for it. Throw us in. God can save us, but even if He doesn't, there's no way we will ever bow down to that thing." So in they went.

As many of you know, the story has a happy ending. The three make it. King Neby goes from one emotional ditch to another. Now he's praising the God of these three. Ah, the fickleness of man. But there's a lesson in here for all of us. Because when the King peered into that fiery furnace, he didn't see just three. He saw four. *"I see four men….the form of the fourth like the Son of God" (Daniel 3:25).* And nothing has changed.

Like then, like now. Today, you may be going through a fiery ordeal. Most likely figuratively rather than literally. Regardless, they're never easy. But He is there. Jesus is with you. For *"lo, I am with you always, even to the end of the age"* (Matthew 28:20). You *will* come out of the fire, and you will be like those three men, *"whose bodies the fire had no power, and the smell of fire was not on them,"* for God *"delivered His servants who trusted in Him"* (Daniel 3:27-28).

Daniel: A Mufasa Sleepover

"So Daniel was taken up out of the den, and no injury whatever was found on him, because he believed in his God" (Daniel 6:23).

Finding envy and jealousy in King Darius's palace court would not have been a strenuous task. No magnifying glass required because, in general, people want what others have. Especially in the upper echelons of power, where coveting is the norm and self-interest rules the day. Now, typically, these just manifest as a cold war within such corridors, with bad behaviors limited to hidden agendas, back-office plotting, slander, scheming, and the occasional figurative backstab. But in Daniel's case? Well, that cold war had turned hot. Diplomacy was over, and now the bullets were flying. Or, more accurately, feeding time had come for some famished lions.

Imagine walking in the shoes of faithful Daniel. Before his first cup of coffee, he arrives at work only to realize the cold war waged against him by his co-workers was suddenly hot. Their boss had signed a decree making it illegal to worship any other god except the King. Do that, and it's off to the lions you go. Love, King Darius. What's an employee to do for the rest of the day? Should he run, hide, or fight? For Daniel, there was no hesitation:

> *"Now when Daniel knew that the writing was signed, he went home. And in his upper room, with his windows open toward Jerusalem, he knelt down on his knees three times that day, and prayed and gave thanks before his God, as was his custom since the early days"* (Daniel 6:10).

Not the UFC or WWE kind of fighting. But the spiritual kind. He went home. Like always. In an upper room where all could see. Like always. With his windows wide open. Like always. Yes, Daniel was a fighter. Like his three friends and their fiery furnace. Nothing stopped these four friends from doing what they had always done. Come what may.

Please note how Daniel's deliverance was achieved. It wasn't because of some ingenious solution he had devised to solve his problem. No, simply *"because he believed in his God."* Other translations use the word *"trusted"* in his God. And ultimately, isn't that what Jesus always asks each of us: "Do you believe Me? Will you trust Me?"

God, give us the grace to trust and believe You. Come what may. Amen.

Daniel: Scary Movies

"My strength left me, my face grew deathly pale, and I felt very weak….
I fainted and lay there with my face to the ground" (Daniel 10:8-9).

Truth be told, I can pretty much track with chapters one through six in the book of Daniel. Very practical, with some incredible stories. But afterward? The bulk of chapters seven through twelve I'll leave to the theologians. Lots of prophetic dreams and visions. Interpretations are not my strong suit. That said, there is one theme that I think is applicable for us all. While these dreams and visions scared Daniel, God's presence provided great relief and comfort to his soul. So if you struggle with disturbing or traumatizing mental images from your past, God's reassurances to Daniel are yours today.

Hear how he described his feelings and emotions after seeing these dreams and visions:

- *"I, Daniel, was troubled by all I had seen, and my visions terrified me" (7:15).*
- *"I, Daniel, was terrified by my thoughts and my face was pale with fear" (7:28).*
- *"While he was speaking, I fainted and lay there with my face to the ground" (8:18).*
- *"My strength left me, my face grew deathly pale, and I felt very weak" (10:8).*

And the response of God (and His Heavenly Hosts) to His terrified servant, Daniel?

- *"And now I am here to tell you what it was, for you are very precious to God" (9:23).*
- *"Just then a hand touched me and lifted me, still trembling, to my hands and knees. And the man said to me, 'Daniel, you are very precious to God'" (10:10-11).*
- *"Then the one who looked like a man touched me again, and I felt my strength returning. "Don't be afraid,' he said, 'for you are very precious to God. Peace! Be encouraged! Be strong!* (10:18-19).

Have you experienced things that have made you troubled, terrified, frightened, or unsettled in your soul? Then God says to you, "Be at peace, be encouraged, and be strong, for you are very precious to Me!" He will never leave you or forsake you, no matter how scary the movie of your life has been or becomes.

A Certain Woman

"A great multitude followed Him and thronged Him... Now a certain woman had a flow of blood for twelve years... she came behind Him in the crowd and touched His garment" (Mark 5:24-25,27).

When I think of brave people in the Bible, I don't typically put *"a certain woman"* near the top of my list. Truth be told, I don't think she even makes honorable mention. Which is probably more of an indictment on my definition of bravery than anything else. With the many stories of sacrifice and valor I've seen or read about over the years, this *"certain woman"* does not neatly fit into any of my courageous categories. And yet, she should.

As a Jewish woman with a chronic twelve-year health issue of blood hemorrhaging, she had been declared unclean by the Law. Meaning everything she touched was also considered unclean. Meaning she could not be around other people – or they, too, would be considered unclean. She was marginalized and a societal outcast, but that would not stop her quest for Jesus.

The multitudes *"thronged"* around Jesus. Think of the President of the United States and the layers of protection his security detail provides. I can imagine this scene with Jesus. His inner circle, disciples, and followers all providing concentric circles of protection from the swarming masses. But that did not thwart this determined woman. No obstacle would prevent her from reaching Jesus.

And her faith! *"For she said, "If only I may touch His clothes, I shall be made well"* (Mark 5:28). She wasn't just thinking it. She was speaking it. *Before* the healing. She was testifying to herself! Her faith was ignited, and she kept speaking that faith out loud. What an example for us. If we want to beat discouragement and defeat in our own lives, a key weapon is to testify to ourselves. Speaking the Word of God to ourselves and over our situation.

And finally, she reached out *"and touched His garment."* In reaching out, she touched not only the Author of the Law but its fulfillment. So, let's learn from this bold, persistent, and brave woman who did not allow anything to keep her from Jesus. No roadblock or obstacle would keep her away from Him who can heal with just one touch.

The Man Born Blind: Sent

"And He said to him, 'Go, wash in the pool of Siloam' (which is translated, Sent). So he went and washed, and came back seeing" (John 9:7).

There are times when God will call us to do the unconventional. Steps of obedience that do not immediately comport with our sense of logic or reason. Take, for instance, the man born blind in John 9. Couldn't Jesus, who spoke the universe into existence, have just uttered the words, and this man would see? Instead, Jesus used dirt and saliva to form clay and pressed it onto his eyes. And if that wasn't enough, Jesus told him to go wash in a pool called Sent. Only then would the blind man see.

In our spiritual journey and relationship with Jesus, obedience is not always easy and sometimes may not make sense. When we get that word, conviction, or prompting from Him, like the clay on the man's eyes, it may initially seem like an irritation. Until, in response to being sent, we go. And then, and often only then, comes sight. For obedience is the great opener of eyes. For the man born blind, and for us.

So let's not argue, fight, defend, or justify our inactivity when God calls us to go. Let's be like Isaiah, when asked by God who will go, replied, *"Here am I! Send me"* (Isaiah 6:8). Not only does obedience provide sight to the ways of the Lord, but it also gives us a boldness we would not otherwise possess. Note how the healed man was not intimidated by the threats of the Pharisees, but bravely declared Jesus to them, *"If this man were not from God, he could do nothing"* (John 9:33).

He did this knowing full well it would lead to his ex-communication from the synagogue, cutting him off from friends and family. While this must have been very painful, the joy of communion and fellowship with Jesus Christ far outweighed any alignment with the Pharisees. Like the blind man, when Jesus tells us to go, may we always respond with a resounding, *"Here am I! Send me."*

The Man Born Blind: Fear

"His parents said these things because they feared the Jews, for the Jews had agreed already that if anyone confessed that He was Christ, he would be put out of the synagogue" (John 9:22).

Fear is a God-given anticipatory or reflexive response to a dangerous, painful, or threatening event. It's our "fight or flight" response. An internal mechanism (via our amygdala) God created in us for survival. While this is all good and necessary, there are times and situations where God calls us to a greater fear, where one fear supersedes and transcends another. Suppose, for instance, you come across a burning house with cries for help from within. If passing by, isn't it our hope we would take the road of heroism, subjugating our fear of fire to our fear for the poor people who may die from it?

Which brings us back to the man born blind in John chapter 9. A family split along the lines of fear. The parents, who had long since reconciled themselves to the fact of their blind son. And a son, now with 20/20 vision. Which fear would transcend the other in the mayhem that would soon commence? For all in Jerusalem lived in an organic social network built upon the foundation of community, with the synagogue as its chief cornerstone. Would fear of social loss drive their decision-making, or would Truth?

In the end, the parents chose their community, while their son chose Jesus. And what do you think emboldened this young man to do so? I would venture to say his sight. With the freshness of his newfound vision, he factually responded to their many questions with innocent simplicity. In doing so, he revealed a far greater fear than the one his parents succumbed to.

Amazing Grace how sweet the sound that saved a wretch like me!
I once was lost but now am found, was blind but now I see.

Peter and John: With Jesus

"Now when they saw the boldness of Peter and John, and perceived that they were uneducated and untrained men, they marveled. And they realized that they had been with Jesus" (Acts 4:13).

God made our minds to form connections. If this, then that. If the car in front of me turns on its right blinker, then it will soon turn right. If my gas mower runs out of gas, then it will stop running. We probably have millions of these connections, most so deeply hidden in our subconscious we don't even realize them. These connections form and create our worldview, developing our take on reality. But what happens when there is a disconnect and our cause-and-effect relationships break? That is called cognitive dissonance. When right blinkers lead to left-hand turns. When red means go, and green means stop. When 1 + 1 = 3. Then hold on! When that happens in increasing measure, unabated confusion will soon give way to full-blown insanity.

Such was the dilemma facing the Sanhedrin in Acts chapter four. They had a connection. If you are educated and trained, then you can boldly teach others. Then along comes Peter and John, creating a massive glitch in their matrix:

> "Wait a minute. These guys are uneducated and untrained. They're just fishermen. They can't teach. We are the ones who should be teaching them. The gall of them to think they can do what only we can do. What seminaries have they attended? What teachers have they sat under? What credentials do they possess? This makes absolutely no sense!"

You're right. It doesn't. Oh, the poor Sanhedrin. Their world was about to be rocked and disrupted. Jesus had scrambled their reality. New cause-and-effect relationships had been created, ones entirely formed by proximity to Him.

The more time we spend with Jesus, drawing closer to Him, the more disruptive we will become to the worldviews around us. This is the transformative effect of being with Jesus, shining His light ever more brightly upon all who are in proximity to us.

Timothy: All Shapes and Sizes

*"And he [Paul] went into the synagogue and spoke boldly for three months...
and this continued for two years, so that all who dwelt in Asia
heard the word of the Lord Jesus Christ, both Jew and Greeks" (Acts 19:8, 10).*

As the head basketball coach of UCLA, John Wooden led the Bruins to 10 national championships in 12 years. When he retired in 1975, how would you like to have been the coach who followed him? Well, Gene Bartow was that lucky guy, but he only lasted 28 months. As he later stated, the pressure of coaching in the shadow of Wooden got to him. "At UCLA, every time you lost it was a major catastrophe." Big shoes are hard to fill.

Consider young Timothy, pastor of the Ephesian church and recipient of two letters written by his mentor, the Apostle Paul. That same bold Paul who wrote the bulk of the New Testament, who shared the gospel with *everyone* in Asia, and the one *"God worked unusual miracles...so that even handkerchiefs or aprons were brought from his body to the sick, and the diseases left them and the evil spirits went out of them"* (Acts 10:11-12). And if that wasn't intimidating enough for Timothy, Ephesus was no pastoral piece of cake. A city devoted to the worship of Diana the fertility goddess, they were quick to riot and attack anyone foolish enough to mess with her revered status (Acts 19).

Wow. Tough act to follow. And a tough job to boot. But wait, it gets worse! Factor in Timothy's temperament: He struggled with insecurity *"Let no one despise your youth"* (1 Tim 4:12), fear *"For God has not given us a spirit of fear"* (2 Tim 1:7), timidity *"do not be ashamed of the testimony of our Lord"* (2 Tim 1:8), and chronic illness *"use a little wine for your stomach's sake and your frequent infirmities"* (1 Tim 5:23). Timothy was no Paul.

And yet, bravery comes in all shapes and sizes. Maybe you can relate more to Timothy than to Paul. A less bold personality given a tough assignment. And yet, like Timothy, you too have a spirit *"of power, of love, and of a sound mind"* (2 Tim 1:7), so you can *"be strong in the grace that is in Christ Jesus"* (2 Tim 2:1).

No matter whom you are following, Christ is with you. No matter the difficulty you're facing, Christ is sufficient. No matter your personality, *"My grace is sufficient for you, for My strength is made perfect in weakness" (1 Cor 12:9)*. And Paul's last words to Timothy are his to you, *"The Lord Jesus Christ be with your spirit. Grace be with you. Amen"* (2 Tim 4:22).

Profiles of the Brave
Our Encouragement

*"Elijah was a man with a nature like ours
[with the same physical, mental, and spiritual limitations
and shortcomings], and he prayed intensely for
it not to rain, and it did not rain on the earth for
three years and six months" (James 5:17 AMP).*

"Here I was worrying about my journey, while God
was helping me all the way. It made me realize that
I am very weak; my courage only borrowed from Him,
but, oh, the peace that flooded my soul... because
I know that He never faileth. I would not, if I could,
turn back now, because I believe that God is
going to reveal Himself in a wonderful way."

Gladys Aylward

Our Encouragement

To state the obvious, life is hard and frequently discouraging. Our plans go awry so quickly. What began as a simple DIY project has become a bottomless money pit. That ideal job turned out, wasn't. The singleness seems to last forever, while the marriage entered into wasn't the bliss imagined. Parenting, which began with such high hopes, has evolved into sadness as the child, now an adult, has set off in a different direction. Those friends we thought would always be there, aren't. Moreover, so many of our prayers have apparently gone unnoticed. These are but a few of the seemingly infinite adversities and quandaries we each face in life. Don't we all need a little – I mean a lot of – encouragement? I know I do.

Where do you find inspiration and encouragement amidst it all? Yes, first and foremost, from God and His Word. But then where? While we're all so different, it does seem to me there is one common place we can look to strengthen our resolve and give us hope to face each day: The biographies and autobiographies of those who have faithfully gone before. Why there? Well, if I'm completely honest, deep down, I think I have a bias towards those in the Bible. I mean, don't you think they had an advantage? So many of them saw Jesus, audibly heard God, or physically walked with Him. Right there, game over. Unfair advantage. That's never happened in my life.

But, of course, I do need them. I desperately need everything and everyone in the Bible. But I also need those who I believe are "just like me." Normal, everyday, real people. The kind you know at work or in your neighborhood. For in these stories, we meet ones who believed an infinite God could, and would, do infinite things. Ones who simply took God at His Word. Men and women of simple, child-like faith, yet lived lives of boldness and courage. For me, I find that so encouraging! Their big God is mine as well. I can because He can. And so can you.

So, yes, I love biographies and autobiographies. I love to read about these very normal people who did such abnormal things by the power of God—mighty, extraordinary exploits accomplished through the ordinary who had surrendered to Him. Like them, you too can experience the God of the impossible, the One who empowers you to do the same. So be encouraged. Through God, you shall do valiantly!

> "What then shall we say to these things? If God is for us, who can be against us? He who did not spare His own Son, but delivered Him up for us all, how shall He not with Him also freely give us all things?" (Romans 8:31-32).

Gladys Aylward: The Small Woman

"In the day when I cried out, You answered me, and made me bold with strength in my soul" (Psalm 138:3).

In the late 1920s, Gladys Aylward was a maid in London but wanted to be a missionary in China. When Jeannie Lawson, a 73-year-old missionary in China, called for a younger woman to help her, Gladys jumped at the chance. Alone and with her life savings in hand, she set out for China in 1930, at the time engaged in war with Russia. Surviving many dangers and difficulties, she finally found Jeannie in Northern China's wild, mountainous area.

There was a men's prison in the area, and the prisoners were rioting, killing each other to the point the soldiers were afraid to go in. The governor of the prison asked Gladys to go in, since she had told everyone she had the living God inside her and He protected her. Terrified, she went in anyway and saw bodies and blood everywhere. One of the convicts came running at her, swinging a large ax. She told him to give it to her, and he did. All the other prisoners stopped in shock, and order was restored. Gladys would return many times to that prison to tell them about Jesus.

Soon, Japan invaded China in 1937, and bombs nearly destroyed Glady's mission. She was kicked and beaten unconscious by soldiers. Still, she remained, caring for wounded people, orphans, and refugees. She would have to flee, along with 100 orphans under her care, as the Japanese approached to kill them. With a reward for her capture, Gladys and the children escaped, having no money and little food. For many days they would travel through enemy territory, the entourage of children aged four to fifteen. Eventually, overcoming impossible odds by the grace of God, the children were delivered safely to an orphanage outside the warzone.

In 1958, Hollywood produced a film about her life called *The Inn of the Sixth Happiness,* drawing from Alan Burgess's biography *The Small Woman.* May her courage be our inspiration. Warriors come in all shapes and sizes, for God's arm is never too short to save. With Him, we can, for He is able. In light of His greatness, like Gladys, may we never say no because of fear. Limitations within and obstacles without are like dust to God. If we could talk to Gladys now, I suspect she would say, *"Oh, magnify the Lord with me, and let us exalt His name together!"* (Psalm 34:3).

David Livingstone: "Dr. Livingstone, I presume?"

"For in this the saying is true: 'One sows and another reaps'" (John 4:37).

Have you ever been discouraged because of the lack of visible fruit in your life? Or maybe you've felt guilty or condemned as you compare yourself with those other "amazing" Christians who lead so many to the Lord, have apparently perfect families, or through whom God seems to do so much. If you can relate, then the life of David Livingstone is for you.

More than 100 books have been written about the best-known missionary ever. Hollywood even produced a movie about him in 1939. Yet, in his life, David Livingstone led only one man to Jesus, and that one man eventually turned his back on Christ. Having arrived in Africa in 1841, he saw no visible fruit for his 32 years of ministry despite traveling over 40,000 miles across the continent to bring the love of Jesus to others.

And let me tell you, his time there was no stroll in the park. Many times, he narrowly escaped charging buffaloes and elephants, 1000-pound crocodiles, enormous pythons, raging hippos, and the spears of natives who assumed he was a hated slave trader. If he wasn't in immediate danger of losing his life, then he was constantly facing unimaginable difficulties. In the desert, he trudged through blistering heat. In the jungles, he waded through marshes and walked in rain daily. Disease-carrying insects and foul water made him sick again and again with malaria and dysentery, diseases that would eventually claim his life in 1873. And yet, until his dying day, on he went, compelled by the love of Jesus to be His ambassador to the Africans he so dearly loved.

In the end, God does not say, "Well done, good and successful servant." He says, "Well done, good and faithful servant." Our job is to be faithful. The results are up to Him. Like the sower in Mark chapter 4, our job is to cast the seed. What soil it lands in and what growth subsequently occurs—well, that's up to God.

Be encouraged. Your finish line on earth is not God's finish line. The seeds you have scattered in your life will produce fruit, whether you see it or not. Because the power is in the seed. Not in you. And not in what you can see. Long after you are gone, God will still be at work, using what you have scattered to produce the increase only He can achieve.

Today, 275 million Africans call themselves Christians.

Charles Colson: The Courage to Confess

"If we say that we have no sin, we deceive ourselves, and the truth is not in us. If we confess our sins, He is faithful and just to forgive us our sins and cleanse us from all unrighteousness" (1 John 1:8-9).

There's a big difference between confession and getting caught. Unfortunately, it's become commonplace today to see a public figure standing at a microphone, flanked by their family, admitting fault. But only *after* it was revealed in the latest video or bombshell report. An admission of guilt in response to the ironclad visibility of their sin. But to be the one to initiate? When nobody knows the secret, and admission may have catastrophic consequences? In a society where we believe *image is everything*, and the chief question asked is, "What's in it for me?" Especially when the impact is reputational, relational, or financial. How rare it is to have someone voluntarily step forward and make what is hidden visible.

Charles Colson was that exception. Known as the "hatchet man" for President Nixon, Colson once said he would step over his grandmother if she got in his way. A tough Marine, Colson was known for his aggressiveness and callous disregard for others. Colson stridently maintained his innocence while fighting the Senate committee investigating the Watergate scandal of the 1970s. Until, that is, he came to Christ. From that point on, he just wanted to tell the truth. To the point where he offered evidence to the prosecution so they could convict him. Pleading guilty to an offense he hadn't been initially charged with, Colson wanted desperately to pay the earthly penalty for his past sins, which he did—seven months in Alabama's Maxwell Prison.

It takes courage to confess what is currently concealed. But if God's glory and truth are your supreme earthly obsessions, all else will pale in comparison, regardless of the consequences. As Nancy DeMoss Wolgemuth wrote:

> "You and I exist for one reason alone: to bring God glory. We were created for His pleasure. If I fixate on how all of this affects *me—my* my comforts, my desires, my fulfillment, my security, my need—then I have made 'myself' an idol. But this is not about *me*. It is about denying self and crowning Christ as Lord, seeking His glory and pleasure above all else. Pleasing Him is truly life's greatest pleasure."

John Testrake: Hijacked

*"God is our refuge and strength, a very present help in trouble,
therefore we will not fear" (Psalm 46:1-2).*

Unexpected trouble. Abrupt danger. Sudden terror. Where a routine day turns into a life-altering event. How will we respond in the moment? Will we panic and fear, or will we be strong and courageous? While we may never have to face such a traumatizing experience in our lives, it would be wise to prepare as though we will. How so?

John Testrake was the pilot of TWA flight 847 from Athens to Rome on June 14, 1985. Having just kissed his wife goodbye, they were looking forward to the anniversary cruise they were about to go on. But that day in June wouldn't be like all the others. Armed Shiite terrorists hijacked the plane, and for two weeks, they sat at Beirut International Airport. Each day, Testrake was held at gunpoint in the cockpit, a gun pressed up against his neck, with the hijackers threatening to blow up the plane if their demands were not met. When they weren't, the terrorists executed an American sailor and dumped his lifeless body onto the tarmac. Day after day, the American public sat mesmerized by this life-and-death drama unfolding in Lebanon. Finally, the last passengers and crew members, including John Testrake, were released unharmed.

Millions of Americans who followed the ordeal on the nightly news considered him a hero. His calm demeanor and strong faith prevented an extremely dangerous situation from becoming more tragic. In his many interviews, John gave glory to God, saying the thing he remembered most about his experience was the constant presence of Jesus, who comforted him, kept him from being afraid, and gave Him hope. In fact, John recounted how he and his flight engineer had church daily: singing hymns, reading the Bible, and praying together.

How would we respond in a similar situation? None of us really knows for sure. But we can prepare, just as John did before that eventful day in June. How? By going to church. Not just on Sunday but every day. Like him, we can daily experience the presence of Christ through worship and praise, reading His Word, and prayer. While there are no guarantees for a smooth and tranquil life here on earth, there is one guarantee: His presence when we're in trouble.

"Therefore, we will not fear."

George Muller: The Courage to Trust

"A father to the fatherless, a defender of widows, is God in His holy habitation"
(Psalm 68:5).

While pastoring a church in Bristol, England, in 1838, George Muller was reading the above verse in Psalm 68 when he had the thought, "If God provides for the fatherless, then all I need to do to help them is be the man God uses to meet their needs." Later, he was further inspired by a man named August Franke, who trusted God to help him care for nearly two thousand orphans. So, for the next six decades, Muller would establish 117 schools and care for over 120,000 orphans and street children, raising the equivalent of $129 million in today's dollars. And yet, he never asked for a cent (or, more accurately, a shilling). Not once. He only prayed, believing God was able.

For example, one morning, Muller awoke to the news that the orphanage, which housed 300 children at the time, had no food. Muller instructed the housemother to seat all the children in the dining room. In front of them all, he thanked God for the food. Then they waited for God to provide. Within a few minutes, a baker knocked on the door. "Mr. Muller," he confessed, "last night, I could not sleep. Somehow, I knew that you would need bread this morning. I got up and baked three batches for you. I will bring it in." A few minutes later, there was another knock on the door. This time, it was the milkman whose cart had broken down in front of the orphanage. "The milk will spoil by the time the cart is fixed," the milkman explained, "so would the children like some free milk?"

A life of faith is not for the faint of heart. Daily, God asks us, "Do you trust Me?" When we're circumstantially blind, when we receive a grave diagnosis, when the money runs out, or when the wayward child does not return home, is He still able? Or are His promises only true in the light, their validity diminishing as the darkness descends?

King Jehoshaphat's words of encouragement and worship are God's words to us today. Words of courage he spoke to his people as the darkness of their enemies descended upon them:

> *"'Believe in the Lord your God, and you shall be established; believe His prophets, and you shall prosper.' And he appointed those who should sing to the Lord, and who should praise the beauty of holiness, as they went out before the army….'*
> (2 Chronicles 20:20-21).

George Muller: A Faith That Will Not Shrink

"And the apostles said to the Lord, 'Increase our faith'" (Luke 17:5).

I believe the crux of the Christian life is this: Will we walk by sight... or faith? For at some point, life *will* close in. It always does. The money is about to run out. Or does. A close relationship breaks. The economy tanks. War looms on the horizon. Unemployment continues with no end in sight. A wayward child remains so despite years of prayer.

Even though he was never invited, fear is constantly knocking on the door of our lives. And predictably, he always brings his two favorite main courses: worry and anxiety. The question is, will we answer the door and let him in?

George Muller was once asked about his ability to trust God in crises. He replied:

> "My faith is the same faith which is found in every believer. It has been increased little by little for the last 26 years. Many times when I could have gone insane from worry, I was at peace because my soul believed the truth of God's promises. God's Word, together with the whole character of God, as He has revealed Himself, settles all questions. His unchangeable love and His infinite wisdom calmed me... It is written, *'He who did not spare His own Son, but delivered Him up for us all, how shall He not with Him also freely give us all things?'"* (Romans 8:32).

William Bathurst was a minister for 32 years in a small village near Leeds, England. He wrote the following:

O for a faith that will not shrink
Though pressed by ev'ry foe
That will not tremble on the brink
Of any earthly woe.

A faith that shines more bright and clear
When tempests rage without;
That when in danger knows no fear
In darkness feels no doubt.

Jim Elliot: A Kernel of Wheat

"I tell you the truth, unless a kernel of wheat falls to the ground and dies, it remains only a single seed. But if it dies, it produces many seeds" (John 12:24).

Throughout the Christian life, we see an oft-repeated pattern. The cycle of death and resurrection. Hopes are frequently squashed, only to be raised by the Lord at some other time and in some other form. Dreams become dashed upon the cold rocks of reality, only to find God replacing them with His plan, His hope, and His future for our lives instead (Jeremiah 29:11). For *"to all who mourn in Israel, He will give a crown of beauty for ashes, a joyous blessing instead of mourning, festive praise instead of despair"* (Isaiah 61:3). Only Jesus Christ can create true beauty from true ashes.

And yet, for much of life, here we might only experience…. death. Resurrection being reserved for there.

From an early age, Jim Elliot wanted to be a missionary, so he studied Greek to translate the Bible into different languages. After graduating from Wheaton College, the more he learned about a Stone Age tribe in Ecuador known as the Aucas, the more he believed God wanted him to go there. The Aucas lived deep in the Amazon jungle and killed anyone who came into their territory. For months, Jim and his four missionary friends made overtures of friendship with the Aucas, first from the air and then from the ground. After making friendly contact with three Aucas, the excited missionaries radioed their wives at base camp the next day, saying they had spotted a group of men heading toward their camp. Their wives would never hear from them again, for they were all ambushed and killed by wooden spears on January 8, 1956.

Here, Jim Elliot just saw death. His own. A kernel of wheat that fell into the ground and died. To many, it seemed like a senseless waste of a promising young life. But in Christ, death is never the end, but the beginning. Both here, and there. For only God can count the number of lives impacted for eternity by Jim Elliot since that fateful day in 1956. To quote him:

"He is no fool who gives what he cannot keep
to gain what he cannot lose."

Corrie Ten Boom: Our Hiding Place

"You are my hiding place; You shall preserve me from trouble; You shall surround me with songs of deliverance" (Psalm 32:7).

Corrie Ten Boom was born in Haarlem, Holland, on April 15th, 1892. She was Holland's first licensed female watchmaker, following in her father's footsteps in helping him run the family clock business. In May of 1940, when the Germans invaded her country, her family saw how the Jews were being treated, so they began hiding the persecuted. On February 28th, 1944, a Dutch informant betrayed the Ten Booms. Arrested, Corrie was kept in solitary confinement until eventually shipped off to the Ravensbrück concentration camp. Huddled in barracks with hundreds of others, sharing mattresses infested with lice, they would rise for roll call at 4 am, forced to work long days with frequent beatings by the guards watching over them. Throughout it all, the smell of dead bodies from the crematorium permeated the camp.

With her family killed at the hands of the Nazis, Corrie was released on December 31st, 1944 due to a clerical error. The next week, all the women her age were sent to the gas chamber.

Corrie would spend the rest of her life spreading the love of Jesus and the forgiveness found in Him. Here are some wise truths from Corrie, a life hidden in Christ:

> "Worrying doesn't empty tomorrow of its sorrow, it empties today of its strength."

> "Forgiveness is an act of the will, and the will can function regardless of the temperature of the heart."

> "You can never learn that Christ is all you need, until Christ is all you have."

Brother Andrew: God's Smuggler

"Wake up! Strengthen what remains and is about to die" (Revelation 3:2).

Brother Andrew, born Anne van der Biji in 1928 in the Netherlands, experienced first-hand oppression under the Nazi regime and then watched the spread of communism immediately following.   While preparing to become a missionary, he read the above verse in Revelation and concluded God was calling him to take God's Word to the believers behind the atheistic Iron Curtain. At the height of the Cold War, when possessing a Bible was illegal, he began fearlessly smuggling Bibles into these countries in his blue Volkswagen Beetle. Approaching heavily guarded border checkpoints, Brother Andrew would pray,

> "Lord, in my luggage I have Scripture I want to take to Your children. When You were on earth, You made blind eyes see. Now, I pray, make seeing eyes blind. Do not let the guards see those things You do not want them to see."

God would answer his prayer. Many times over. In fact, once when he approached the Romanian border, he watched the guards spend over an hour meticulously searching cars in front of him. Removing hubcaps, seats, and engine parts. Realizing no cleverness on his part would keep the Bibles from being discovered, he took what Bibles he had and spread them out over the interior in plain sight and prayed his miracle-believing prayer. When his turn came, the guard looked at his passport, glanced around, and waved him through.

You may not be called to smuggle Bibles into countries hostile to Christians, but God is calling you to a life of faith. A life of courage, believing He can, He is able, and He will. A life of expectancy in His goodness, replacing fear with faith in a Sovereign God and His all-powerful Word.

Andrea Ashley: Why Not Me?

"And the things that you have heard from me among many witnesses, commit these to faithful men who will be able to teach others also" (2 Timothy 2:2).

To encourage is to give courage, and one of the most effective ways to encourage other believers is through life-upon-life mentoring. Here, in the above verse, we see four generations of discipleship: Paul, Timothy, faithful men, and others. When I (Marjie) was in college, my mentor, Andrea Ashley, profoundly modeled this for me.

2 Timothy 2:2 was Andrea's life verse. She lived it out every moment of every day in the college town in which we lived. She had ample access to influence the lives of young college students, of which I was a grateful recipient. Andrea showed me how serious the claims of Christ really are. At each meeting together, our conversation always centered on the Word. She would share in the context of her testimony and her changed life – often weeping for what Jesus had done for her.

Then she would challenge me with the Word, having me dig in and find the truth for myself, asking me what it meant and how I would apply it. At our follow-up meeting, she would hold me accountable for what she had taught me the time before. She often said, "We don't have all kinds of time." Meaning, utilize and embrace each day with eternity in mind. The impartation of her life into mine created brave enthusiasm to do the same in others as God multiplied His kingdom on that college campus.

Andrea had a deep spiritual water table, a reservoir that enabled her to walk through her cancer journey. One that would ultimately claim her life. As she battled the disease for many years, she never asked, "Why me?" Her question was always, "Why not me?" Like Paul, she knew she had been called and equipped to do the work of the Gospel. She knew where she was going, having complete confidence that, in the end, she'd already won through Jesus Christ. She used her cancer journey to take the Gospel to every nurse, doctor, and person she met along the way.

Andrea raised my spiritual water table. I am the fruit of Andrea Ashley's life. So let me ask you, how's your spiritual water table? Who's your Paul, or better yet, who's your Timothy? Who are you coming alongside and encouraging? Like Andrea, you too can boldly and bravely assert, "Why not me?"

Hudson Taylor: Trust

"Commit your way to the Lord; trust in Him and He will do this: He will make your righteousness shine like the dawn, the justice of your cause like the noonday sun"
(Psalm 37:5-6).

Before he was born in 1832, Hudson Taylor's parents prayed their son would be a missionary to China. Twenty-two years later, that prayer was answered. Upon arriving, Hudson's faith would be tested again and again. He was alone among thousands of people who looked at him with dislike and suspicion. He witnessed and preached for many months with no results. And yet, he found strength in trusting God in prayer. As he later shared with friends, "Depend upon it. God's work, done in God's way, will never lack God's supplies."

Going deeper into the country, he fell in love with an English girl who worked in a mission and married her. But after six years in the country, he became gravely ill and needed to return to England with his wife and child. But his heart was with the Chinese, so he translated the Bible into Chinese and prayed for 24 more missionaries to join him in China. When no missionary societies in England would support him, Hudson created his own, The China Inland Mission. Hudson then returned with his family and this new team. However, more hardship awaited him. His eldest child died, and then his 33-year-old wife died soon after giving birth, along with their newborn son. The money ran out, and many of the new missionaries resisted him over his methods. And yet, through it all, Hudson's faith grew, and God answered his prayers. As he wrote a friend, "We have 27 cents and all the promises of God."

He went back to England and prayed for 70 more missionaries. He never asked for money, but money poured in, and 70 new missionaries left for China. He asked God for 100, and 102 set sail the following year. When the Boxer Rebellion broke out in 1900, many of these missionaries were killed. When Hudson heard of their plight, he was grief-stricken and wrote, "I cannot read, I cannot pray, I can scarcely even think – but I can trust."

At the time of his death at age 72, there were 849 missionaries in China and 125,000 Chinese Christians. While we may never be missionaries or start a missionary society, we can be assured God's work, done God's way, will never lack God's supplies. If it's God's will, then it's God's bill. That's His promise to us, so we, like Hudson, can always trust Him for it. For each of us, in Christ, have "all the promises of God."

The Shackleton Expedition
Now Hiring

"If you faint in the day of adversity, your strength is small" (Proverbs 24:10).

It was early 1914. World War I had just begun, and polar expeditions were a global obsession. In an attempt to reach the South Pole, Robert Scott and Ernest Shackleton failed in 1902 and 1909, respectively. Roald Amundsen succeeded in 1911, and now Shackleton wants to be the first person to traverse Antarctica, landing at the tip of South America while exiting on the other side near Australia. To identify his needed crew, an ad was run in a London newspaper that read:

> "Men wanted for hazardous journey, small wages, bitter cold, long months of complete darkness, constant danger, safe return doubtful. Honor and recognition in case of success."

If Jesus Christ had posted a similar ad for His work crew, it might have read something like this:

> "Men and women wanted for the difficult task of building My church. You will often be misunderstood, frequently by those working with you. You will face constant attacks from an invisible enemy. You will most likely see little results from your labor, and your full reward will not come until your work is fully completed. It may cost you your home, your ambitions, and potentially even your life."

Would you have answered that job posting? Personally, I was oblivious to the costs involved in following Christ. I just knew my life was a hot mess, and something was missing. But for many others, they knew exactly what the cost would entail. *"If anyone comes to Me and does not hate father and mother, wife and children, brothers and sisters – yes, even their own life—such a person cannot be my disciple"* (Luke 14:26). Such is the call of Christ. Adversity, trouble, and trials await us. But Jesus is greater, and His presence and grace will *always* be sufficient for any task He writes in our job description.

The Shackleton Expedition
Not On Your Vision Board

"Joseph, who was sold as a slave, they bruised his feet with fetters and placed his neck in an iron collar" (Psalm 105:17-18).

A polar expedition in 1914 was no picnic. The mean annual temperature at the South Pole is around *negative* 60 degrees. The average wind speed is 23 mph, with gusts over 100 mph. And if the elements weren't enough, stories about failed expeditions would certainly exclude the faint of heart from applying. Captain Charles Hall was poisoned by his men on the Polaris expedition to the North Pole in 1871. Admiral Robert Peary was accused of "intolerant brutality" and the reason for suicides on his expeditions in the 1890's. And explorer Adolphus Greely lost 19 of 25 men and was accused of cannibalism.

Yet, Ernest found his intrepid crew of 28, and off they went. On December 5, 1914, the *Endurance* set sail from South Georgia Island. But like so many before them, things didn't go quite as planned. On January 18, 1915, the ship became trapped in pack ice just a day's sail from the intended landing site. No satellites. No drones. No internet. No cell phone coverage. Nobody knew of their predicament. The crew would spend the next 10 months trapped on the ice, retrieving necessities from the ship, until finally, the *Endurance* would be completely crushed and sink to the bottom of the sea.

Joseph had a dream, too. In fact, he had several of them (Genesis 37). But there was no straight line for him between those dreams and their fulfillment. Slavery, fetters, and iron collars would first be his fate. Maybe you're in a similar place where your dreams are, at best, unfulfilled and, at worst, crushed beneath the pack ice of life. If this is you and your season of life, may you find your rest and peace where Joseph found his. In the abiding presence of Jesus. *"But the Lord was with Joseph, and showed him mercy, and gave him favor in the sight of the keeper of the prison"* (Genesis 39:21). Life can be so very difficult, yet His presence is your confidence that all is, and will be, well with your soul.

The Shackleton Expedition
Playing Soccer on Pack Ice

"The Lord was with Joseph, and he was a successful man...and his master saw that the Lord was with him. So Joseph found favor in his sight, and served him"
(Genesis 39:2, 4).

Let's put ourselves in the shoes of Shackleton and his crew. Hopelessly trapped, our only shelter (the ship) is slowly being crushed by the moving ice. The food supply will soon be gone, and no one knows about our predicament, nor will anyone come to our rescue. How would we react? Would we be like all those other failed expeditions and their gruesome tales? Or would we take a path less traveled, one that makes no sense given the circumstances, even with reality constantly screaming in our faces, "Give up!"

If you were to observe the cover of the book *Shackleton's Way*, you would see a most unusual and counter-intuitive photograph. With the Endurance in the background getting crushed by the ice, the men in the foreground are playing soccer. Yes, soccer. They had built a couple of crude goals from some sticks, and there they were, kicking around a ball as if they didn't have a care in the world. No suicides. No cannibalism. Just the opposite. Having fun with their friends on the ice in negative 60-degree weather.

A critical truth for thriving amid insurmountable odds is the company you keep while in it. Make it a point not to have Eeyore's on your shortlist. Heavy trials require courage, and a primary source for that comes from en**courage**ment. When weariness and discouragement are our constant companions, we all need contrarian voices. Like the company of God's presence as He speaks to you through His Word. Like the company of Shackleton was to his friends:

> "I always found him rising to his best and inspiring confidence when things were at their blackest." *Frank Hurley, photographer, Endurance*

> "No matter what turns up, he is always ready to alter his plans and make fresh ones, and in the meantime laughs, jokes, and enjoys a joke with anyone, and in this way keeps everyone's spirits up." *Frank Worley, captain, Endurance*

The Shackleton Expedition
Game Over (?)

"Yet the chief butler did not remember Joseph, but forgot him. Then it came to pass, at the end of two full years, that Pharaoh had a dream" (Genesis 40:23-41:1).

With the sinking of the Endurance, having spent 10 months trapped on the pack ice, the crew would spend another 5 ½ months living in tents on that same floating ice, dragging their three lifeboats along as they hopped to safety from one sheet of ice to another. On April 9, 1916, the men set off into the tumultuous sea and landed on Elephant Island two weeks later. Shackleton and six companions then left the rest of the crew behind, sailing 800 miles in the *James Caird* in an attempt to seek help. Sixteen days later (slowed down by a hurricane), they reached South Georgia Island... but landed on the wrong side! They would have to hike nearly 40 miles over a glacier mountain pass before finding civilization.

When trapped in a difficult trial, time seems to slow down. Maybe even stop. If the adage "time flies when you're having fun" is true, the opposite is true also. As the seemingly endless trial plods along, it's easy for hopelessness to set in. I'm sure Joseph had to wrestle with such hopelessness. Hated and forsaken by his siblings, then unjustly accused and sent to prison, he is now forgotten for *"two full years."* How long that must have seemed to the one who had merely shared his dreams and now was abandoned to a trial going from bad to worse.

No promise in the Bible assigns a set day and time for deliverance from our trial. The closest may be 1 Peter 5:6, which says He will deliver us *"in due time."* Soon. In just a bit. A little while longer. When the time is right. Not exactly what our impatient hearts want to hear. And yet, while we seek *what* we want, Christ seeks *who* He wants, for Christ wants you. So cast *"all your care upon Him, for He cares for you"* (1 Peter 5:7). And then, in His perfect time, He will do what only He can do:

> *"But may the God of all grace, who called us to His eternal glory by Christ Jesus, after you have suffered a while, perfect, establish, strengthen, and settle you. To Him be the glory and the dominion forever and ever. Amen"* (1 Peter 5:10-11).

The Shackleton Expedition
What are the Odds?

"So now it was not you who sent me here, but God" (Genesis 45:8).

Yesterday, we mentioned in passing that Shackleton and six companions then left the rest of the crew behind, sailing 800 miles in the James Caird in an attempt to seek help. Sixteen days later (slowed down by a hurricane), they reached South Georgia Island. Wait. What?? No GPS. No radio communications. No Coast Guard. No gas motor. Just stars and the sun to guide them? One degree off in their calculations, and they and the entire crew back on Elephant Island would have perished. Many experts and historians say the odds were significantly less than 1% of making it to that island given the monstrous swells, freezing temperatures, limited supplies, health condition of the men, and a hurricane thrown in for good measure.

In the trials of your life, do you give yourself similar odds of making it? Especially when that trial keeps going on and on, getting heavier by the day? Beyond what any sane person would ever dial up for themselves? Why would God do that? Doesn't it seem, at times, like cruel and unusual punishment?

Like Shackleton, Paul and his companions were in a similar hopeless predicament. *"We were burdened beyond measure, above strength, so that we despaired even of life. Yes, we had the sentence of death in ourselves…"* (2 Corinthians 1:8, 9a). Filled with despair, Paul thought he was going to die. God had given him far more than he could handle. But why? *"… that we should not trust in ourselves but in God who raises the dead…" (v. 9b).* Unimaginable adversity had taught Paul the *why*.

The crushing loads of life are to point us up to Him. For all of life is about our increasing dependency on Him, and the hotter the crucible, the more likely the dross of unbelief will be burned off, enabling our faith, *"of greater worth than gold,"* to shine with ever-increasing brightness. With increasing faith, we'll trust the One whose odds are always 100%. Past, present, and future: *"…who delivered us from so great a death, and does deliver us; in whom we trust that He will still deliver us" (v. 10).* Great is His faithfulness!

The Shackleton Expedition
Deliverance

"But as for you, you meant evil against me; but God meant it for good"
(Genesis 50:20).

Having found a whaling village after their glacial hike across South Georgia island, Shackleton and his team would experience more failures before successfully rescuing his crew left behind on Elephant Island. Kiernan Mulvaney provides the following account:

"This final task in many ways proved to be the most trying and time-consuming of all. The first ship on which Shackleton set out ran dangerously low on fuel while trying to navigate the pack ice, and was forced to turn back to the Falkland Islands. The government of Uruguay proffered a vessel that came within 100 miles of Elephant Island before being beaten back by the ice.

But Shackleton procured a third ship, the Yelcho, from Chile; and finally, on August 30, 1916, the saga of the Endurance and its crew came to an end. The men on the island were settling down to a lunch of boiled seal's backbone when they spied the Yelcho just off the coast. It had been 128 days since the James Caird had left; within an hour of the Yelcho appearing, all ashore had broken camp and left Elephant Island behind. Twenty months after setting out for the Antarctic, every one of the Endurance crew was alive and safe."

Bravery. Courage, Resilience. These attributes characterized every crew member of the aptly named *Endurance.* Like them, may we finish strong and *"run with endurance the race that is set before us, looking unto Jesus, the author and finisher of our faith"* (Hebrews 12:1,2).

"You wait. Everyone has an Antarctic."
Thomas Pynchon, crew member, Endurance

The Shackleton Expedition
Lessons in Leadership

"And Pharaoh was angry with his two officers...so he put them in the prison... and the captain of the guard charged Joseph with them, and he served them" *(Genesis 40:2-4).*

In Ernest Shackleton, we have a tangible example of servant leadership. Like Joseph was to the butler and baker in the above verse, and like Jesus was to his disciples, *"Jesus...rose from supper...poured water into a basin and began to wash the disciples' feet"* (John 13:3-5). Here are quotes about Shackleton, the leader, from those who knew him best:

> "He didn't care if he went without a shirt on his own back, so long as the men he was leading had sufficient clothing. He was a wonderful man in that way; you thought the party mattered more than anything else." *Lionel Greenstreet, first officer, Endurance*

> "He [Shackleton] was essentially a fighter, afraid of nothing and of nobody, but withal he was human, overflowing with kindness and generosity, affectionate, and loyal to all his friends." *Louis Bernacchi, physicist, Discovery*

Frank Wild, Shackleton's second in command aboard the *Endurance*, also tells the story of the leadership example he set on an earlier expedition. The crew was on the brink of starvation. Waking Wild up, Shackleton insisted he eat one of the few remaining biscuits. When Wild refused, Shackleton threatened to bury it in the snow rather than eat it himself. Wild took the biscuit, a gesture he would never forget.

Shackleton embodied a commitment to people all true leaders possess, for he used his authority to serve others, to the point of a willingness to pay the ultimate sacrifice. Just as Jesus did for us, who *"being found in appearance as a man, He humbled Himself and became obedient to the point of death, even death of the cross"* (Philippians 4:8).

Courage Composed
Our Worship

"He will rejoice over you with gladness, He will quiet you with His love, He will rejoice over you with singing"

(Zephaniah 3:17).

"Songs in the night, too, prove that we have true courage. Many sing by day who are silent by night, they are afraid of thieves and robbers; but the Christian who sings in the night proves himself to be a courageous character. It is the bold Christian who can sing God's sonnets in the darkness."

Charles Spurgeon

Our Worship

Singing hymns in church is not cool anymore (Ok, boomer, you're dating yourself by using the word "cool"). Today, at least in America, singing in the church is generally centered around contemporary worship music, recently written worship songs often characterized by a positive, uplifting tone, with lyrics focused on personal praise and thanksgiving to God. While some might take exception to this, for various reasons, I think, on the whole, it's all well and good. May we, as the church, always lift our worship and thanksgiving to God in song as we offer a sacrifice of praise to Him!

That said, I'll be honest. I love the hymns. So, my purpose in including the following stories is twofold. First, please note the lives of the people who wrote them. While we often sing dressed in comfortable clothes, standing in comfortable climate-controlled surroundings, these hymns were forged from the fiery trials of life, from the heartache of pain and suffering.

So may your mental image of these composers not be as though they were dressed in Victorian-era finery, sipping tea in their bedroom as they gazed out upon their vast estate, as might be depicted in one of those BBC historical dramas. No, instead, imagine men and women alone, hovering over their tear-stained poetry in dim candlelight, attempting to put into words the supernatural intimacy they were experiencing in the comfort and consolation of the Living God. These are the backstories of so many of the hymns we sing in our worship of Him.

Second, where and when do we sing? For most of us, the answer to the "where" part of the question is pretty straightforward: In church. Where else would we sing? Well, may I offer something for your consideration: What if we were to sing daily? When we're folding laundry, running errands in the car, or on the way to work. What if singing became just a daily thing, like breathing and eating? Paul does say, *"speaking to one another in psalms and hymns and spiritual songs, singing and making melody in your heart to the Lord"* (Ephesians 5:19). Sounds much more frequently to me than just on Sunday morning for twenty minutes. How might our lives change as a result?

How about the "when" part of our singing? I think the Spurgeon quote at the beginning of this chapter pretty much sums it up. Of course, singing when it's "day" is as natural as the sunlight. I imagine Jule Andrews spinning around in circles on the Alps, singing, "The hills are alive with the sound of music." Singing when all is right with the world is so very natural. But singing when it's "night?" Well, that's a different story. And that's why it's called *"a sacrifice of praise"* (Hebrews 13:15). We're going against our natural inclinations, which is good for us and our souls. So, I encourage you to make singing a regular part of your daily walk with God, regardless of the day or night you might find yourself in.

Joseph Scriven: What a Friend We Have in Jesus

"No longer do I call you servants, for a servant does not know what his master is doing; but I have called you friends, for all things that I heard from My Father I have made known to you" (John 15:15).

Hymns have been sung for centuries in the church. While no longer holding the popularity they once did, there is much to glean from the brave and humble backstories of those who composed them. Frequently, you'll find pain and suffering, coupled with their resilience to it, birthed expressions only a soul in union with Christ could produce. Joseph Scriven was no exception.

Scriven watched in shock as the body of his fiancée was pulled from the lake. Their wedding had been planned for the very next day. Grief-stricken, Joseph left his native Ireland for Canada, hoping to start a new life abroad. There, Joseph fell in love again. But tragedy repeated itself when his bride, Eliza Roche, contracted tuberculosis and died just days before they were to be wed.

To escape his sorrow, Scriven poured himself into the ministry. He lived a simple life in Port Hope, Canada, helping the poor, cutting firewood for widows, and giving away his clothes and money to those in need. Serving others in the obscurity of anonymity, news reached him his mother in Ireland was gravely ill. Not having the funds to help or to be with her, he mailed the following poem to encourage her:

What a Friend we have in Jesus,
all our sins and griefs to bear!
What a privilege to carry,
everything to God in prayer.
Oh, what peace we often forfeit,
oh what needless pain we bear.
All because we do not carry
everything to God in prayer!

Are we weak and heavy laden,
cumbered with a load of care?
Precious Savior, still our refuge!
Take it to the Lord in prayer.
Do thy friends despise, forsake thee?
Take it to the Lord in prayer.
In His arms He'll take and shield thee;
thou wilt find a solace there.

Elizabeth Prentiss: More Love to Thee, O Christ

"It is good for me that I have been afflicted, that I may learn Your statutes"
(Psalm 119:71).

Just a few days before Elizabeth turned nine, her beloved father, Edward, died of tuberculosis. For months, she resented people who tried to help, threw temper tantrums, and tried the patience of her grieving mother. As Elizabeth grew older, she longed to trust God as her parents had, but her personality, given to extremes, would cause her to believe she loved God more than life at one moment, only to plunge into deep despair the next.

She married a minister and had a daughter, Annie, and a son named Eddy. Elizabeth was expecting her third child when Eddy became ill. He died of meningitis three months before the birth of his little sister, Bessie. A month later, Bessie became very sick and would die the next day. Her family had lost two children in the span of five months. In reflecting on this profound season of grief, Elizabeth wrote:

> "My faith was staggered under this new blow, and I blush to tell how hard I find it to say cheerfully, 'Thy will be done.' Oh how I wish, do long to feel an entire, unquestioning submission to Him who pities while He afflicts me."

"To love Christ more," Elizabeth once said, "is the deepest need, the constant cry of my soul…. Out in the woods and on my bed and out driving, when I am happy and busy, and when I am sad and idle, the whisper keeps going up for more love, more love, more love!" Here, in His tender embrace, she found the courage to continue.

Once earthly joy I craved, sought peace and rest.
Now Thee alone I seek; give what is best.
This is all my prayer shall be: More love, O Christ to Thee;
More love to Thee, more love to Thee!

Let sorrow do its work, send grief and pain;
Sweet are Thy messengers, sweet their refrain,
When they can sing with me: More love, O Christ to Thee,
More love to Thee, more love to Thee!

Thomas Chisholm: Great is Thy Faithfulness

"Because of the Lord's faithful love we do not perish, for His mercies never end. They are new every morning: great is Your faithfulness!" (Lamentations 3:22-23).

You don't have to be a superhero to display courage. Anytime you choose inconvenience, step out of your comfort zone, or take a risk, you exhibit bravery. While you may think it entails falling on a grenade to save your platoon, running into a burning building to rescue a family, or free-climbing El Capitan in Yosemite National Park, in reality, courage is far more easily attained by us mere mortals. And you don't even have to drink a Red Bull to do it!

Take, for instance, Thomas Chisholm. Born in a log cabin in Kentucky in 1866, he was educated in a simple country schoolhouse. At age sixteen, he began to teach there. However, he wanted to have a greater impact in life, so at age thirty-six, he served as a Methodist minister. For one year. That's it. Ill health forced him to resign. What would he now do to influence the world for Jesus Christ? He would work at a desk job as a life insurance clerk for the rest of his life. And write poetry on the side. By all accounts, his life was ordinary, unremarkable, and simple. So much for the aspirations of youth.

At least, one would think. When Thomas was almost sixty, he did a very brave thing. He made public what had always been private. His poetry. He sent several of his poems to a friend who worked at a Christian music publisher. The friend, William Runyan, was so moved by one of those poems that he set it to music.

All of us can step out of our comfort zone, do the inconvenient, or take a risk. What is God asking you to do today?

Great is Thy faithfulness, O God my Father,
There is no shadow of turning with Thee;
Thou changest not, Thy compassions they fail not;
As Thou hast been Thou forever wilt be.

Great is Thy Faithfulness!
Great is Thy Faithfulness!
Morning by morning new mercies I see;
All I have needed Thy hand hath provided
Great is Thy faithfulness, Lord unto me!

Philip Bliss: I Will Sing of My Redeemer

"For your name's sake, O Lord, pardon my iniquity, for it is great" (Psalm 25:11).

On December 28, 1876, the hymn writer Philip Bliss and his wife Lucy boarded a train bound for Chicago, where Philip would assist D. L. Moody in his evangelistic campaign. With their train needing to stop for engine repairs, the passengers had to stay in a hotel for a night while their baggage was loaded onto another train and sent ahead to Chicago. The following day, the train departed but was soon caught in a blinding snowstorm, running three hours late as it struggled along. Suddenly, as they crossed a trestle over a swollen river, the bridge gave way, and the train plummeted 75 feet into the icy waters below. Soon, a fire broke out from the coal stoves that served to heat the train cars. All was consumed in the fire, and 92 souls lost their lives that day, including Philip and Lucy Bliss.

Mr. Bliss's trunk reached Chicago safely, and when it was opened, they found the last song he had written before his death, which began as follows, "I know not what awaits me. God kindly veils my eyes." In addition, one of the many songs found in his baggage was the words to *I Will Sing of My Redeemer,* which became a world-famous hymn when music was later added to it by James McGranahan. Here, Bliss expresses his love for Christ and the joyful response of a once-imprisoned soul. The supernatural recipient of a full and complete pardon from the Living God. What it truly means to be set free by Christ.

From *I Will Sing of My Redeemer:*

> *I will sing of my Redeemer and His wondrous love to me;*
> *On the cruel cross He suffered, from the curse to set me free*
> *Sing, O sing of my Redeemer, with His blood He purchased me;*
> *On the cross He sealed my pardon, paid the debt and made me free.*

Horatio Spafford: It Is Well With My Soul

"I have told you these things, so that in Me you may have peace. In this world you will have trouble. But take heart! I have overcome the world" (John 16:33).

On November 21, 1873, Anna Spafford and her four young daughters set sail from the U.S. to Europe on the French ocean liner Ville du Havre. About four days into the crossing, the ship collided with the Scottish ship, the Loch Earn. Within approximately 12 minutes, the Ville du Havre slipped beneath the dark waters of the Atlantic, carrying with it 226 of the 313 passengers, including the four Spafford children. A sailor, rowing a small boat over the spot where the ship went down, spotted a woman floating on a piece of wreckage. It was Anna, still alive. Nine days later, she arrived in Cardiff, Wales, and immediately wired her husband, Horatio, "Saved alone, what shall I do?"

Horatio booked passage on the next available ship and left to join his grieving wife. With the ship about four days out, the captain called Spafford to his cabin and told him they were over the place where his children went down. It was then that Mr. Spafford returned to his cabin and wrote the following hymn:

> *When peace like a river attendeth my way,*
> *when sorrows like sea billows roll*
> *Whatever my lot, Thou hast taught me to say*
> *It is well, it is well with my soul.*
>
> *Though Satan should buffet, though trials should come,*
> *let this blest assurance control,*
> *that Christ hath regarded my helpless estate,*
> *and has shed His own blood for my soul.*
>
> *My sin, oh the bliss of this glorious thought,*
> *my sin not in part but the whole,*
> *is nailed to the cross and I bear it no more,*
> *Praise the Lord, Praise the Lord, O my soul!*
>
> *And Lord, haste the day when my faith shall be sight,*
> *the clouds be rolled back as a scroll:*
> *The trump shall resound, and the Lord shall descend,*
> *even so, it is well with my soul!*

Charlotte Elliott: Just As I Am

*"All that the Father gives Me will come to Me, and the one who comes to Me
I will by no means cast out" (John 6:37).*

With her health broken and imprisoned by her disability, Charlotte Elliott was a very bitter woman. "If God loved me," she would mutter, "He would not have treated me this way." Hoping to help her, a minister named Dr. Cesar Malan visited the Elliotts on May 9, 1822. Over dinner, Charlotte lost her temper and railed against God and her family in a violent outburst. Her embarrassed family left the room, leaving Dr. Malan alone with Charlotte.

"You are tired of yourself, aren't you?" he asked. "You are holding to your hate and anger because you have nothing else in the world to cling to. Consequently, you have become sour, bitter, and resentful."

"What is your cure?" asked Charlotte.

"The faith you are trying to despise."

As they talked, Charlotte softened. "If I wanted to become a Christian and to share the peace and joy you possess," she finally asked, "what would I do?"

Dr. Malan replied, "You would give yourself to God just as you are now, with your fightings and fears, hates and loves, pride and shame."

"I would come to God just as I am? Is that right?"

Charlotte did come just as she was, and her heart changed that very night. She would later write:

> *Just as I am, without one plea,*
> *but that Thy blood was shed for me,*
> *And that Thou bidst me come to Thee,*
> *O Lamb of God, I come, I come!*
>
> *Just as I am, and waiting not,*
> *to rid my soul of one dark blot;*
> *To Thee whose blood can cleanse each spot,*
> *O Lamb of God, I come, I come!*
>
> *Just as I am, though tossed about,*
> *with many a conflict, many a doubt,*
> *Fightings and fears within, without,*
> *O Lamb of God, I come, I come!*

Anne Steele: Desiring Resignation and Thankfulness

"But may the God of all grace, who called us to His eternal glory by Christ Jesus, after you have suffered a while, perfect, establish, strengthen, and settle you"
(1 Peter 5:10).

It's not your typical worship song title, is it? At least to our ears and in our day and age. Unfamiliar to most of us, this once widely sung hymn reminds us of the brave resilience God establishes in us through our suffering.

Born in 1716 in Broughton, England, Anne's mother died when she was only three. At age 19, a severe hip injury made her a lifelong invalid. And at age 21, her fiancé drowned the day before they were to be married. Suffering the bulk of her life with what seems to have been malaria, Anne began writing devotional material as a way to express her intimacy with Christ and His sovereign will for her life:

> *Father, whatever of earthly bliss*
> *Thy sovereign will denies,*
> *Accepted at Thy throne,*
> *let this my humble prayer, arise:*
>
> *Give me a calm and thankful heart,*
> *From every murmur free;*
> *The blessing of Thy grace impart,*
> *And make me live to Thee.*
>
> *Let the sweet hope that Thou art mine*
> *My life and death attend,*
> *Thy presence through my journey shine,*
> *And crown my journey's end.*

The prayer of the final stanza was answered on November 11, 1778, the day of her death. As her weeping friends gathered around, she closed her eyes and whispered her last words: "I know that my Redeemer liveth."

Martin Rinkart: Now Thank We All Our God

"Enter His gates with thanksgiving and His courts with praise;
give thanks to him and praise His name" (Psalm 100:4).

From *The Quiet Place* by Nancy DeMoss Wolgemuth:

Martin Rinkart was a 17th-century Lutheran pastor serving in his hometown of Eilenberg during the height of the Thirty Years' War. A walled city, Eilenberg soon found itself overrun with refugees and injured troops, bringing on not only fear and overcrowding but a deadly wave of disease, pestilence, hunger, and want. The Rinkart home became a makeshift refuge of sorts for many of the sick and stranded. And though limited with hardly enough food and supplies to care for his own family, Martin ministered tirelessly to the needs of those around him. When other pastors fled for safety, he stayed on, eventually conducting more than 4,500 funeral services that year. One of those was for his wife.

And yet at some point amid these dire events, Martin composed a family grace to be said by his children before meals – a hymn still sung today all across Germany at state occasions and national days of remembrance:

"Now thank we all our God,
With hearts and hands and voices,
Who wondrous things hath done,
In whom His world rejoices;
Who from our mother's arms
Hath blessed us on our way
With countless gifts of love,
And still is ours today."

When we sing these words in the comfortable surroundings of a Thanksgiving service at church, we smell turkey in the oven, warm bread on the table. We hear the voices of relatives, enjoying reconnecting and conversing with one another. But make no mistake: this joy-filled refrain wasn't birthed in the settled quiet of a country cottage. It was forged in pain and suffering and grief and death. True Thanksgiving comes at a cost. And no circumstances are so dire that they can't produce hymns of joy and thanks on the lips of those who know their God.

John Newton: Amazing Grace

"In Him we have redemption through His blood, the forgiveness of sins, according to the riches of his grace" (Ephesians 1:7).

Born in 1725, John Newton's mother was a godly influence who devoted herself to nurturing his soul, having him memorize Scripture and the hymns of his day. Unfortunately, she passed away from tuberculosis when John was just seven years of age. After her death, he was raised by his irreligious father, a merchant ship captain. At age eleven, Newton began accompanying him, and would make five sea voyages before he turned eighteen. In 1743, while visiting friends, he was forcibly recruited to serve in the Navy against his will. After desertion and flogging, he eventually was kicked out, traded for another man from a passing merchant ship, a slave vessel.

Newton then began his career in the slave trade. Many dangers, toils, and snares soon followed; skirting death too numerous to count. And in an ironic twist, felled by malaria, the West African Sherbro tribe abducted Newton and made him a slave to their abusive princess. Rescued by an English captain, Newton quickly went back to engaging in and profiting from the slave trade, making three voyages as captain of a slave ship.

While at sea, it was a sudden storm on March 9, 1748, that caused him to cry out to God for mercy. Moments after he left the deck, his replacement was swept overboard. Throughout the tumult, he realized his helplessness and concluded only the grace of God could save him. Later, he would write:

> "That tenth of March is a day much remembered by me, and I have never suffered it to pass unnoticed since the year 1748 – the Lord came from on high and delivered me out of deep waters."

Years later, he would pen a poem to accompany his 1773 New Year's Day sermon entitled "Faith's Review and Expectations," based on 1 Chronicles 17:16-17:

> *Amazing grace! How sweet the sound!*
> *That saved a wretch like me!*
> *I once was lost, but now am found;*
> *Was blind but now I see.*
>
> *Thro' many dangers, toils and snares*
> *I have already come.*
> *'Tis grace that brought me safe thus far,*
> *And grace will lead me home.*

Works Cited

Nicholas Whipps Ed. D, "Bend, Don't Break," LinkedIn, posted July 13, 20213, accessed July 31, 22024, https://www.linkedin.com/pulse/bend-dont-break-nicholas-whipps-ed-d-

Cillea Houghton, "The Rebellious Meaning Behind Alice Cooper's Signature Hit," American Songwriter, posted July 27, 2023, accessed accessed August 2, 2024, https://americansongwriter.com/the-rebellious-meaning-behind-alice-coopers-signature-hit-schools-out/

Alice Cooper, "Alice Cooper's School's Out and Other Deluxe Editions," Alice Cooper.com, posted April 23, 2023, accessed on August 2, 2024, https://alicecooper.com/alice-cooper-schools-out-and-killer-deluxe-editions/

OttawaLife Contributor, "Putting the Science in Science Fiction – Violet Incredible," OttawaLife, posted December 13, 2012, accessed August 12, 2024, https://www.ottawalife.com/article/putting-the-science-in-science-fiction-violet-incredible/

Stephen Kelly, "Inside the cutting-edge neuroscience that could create real-life Star Wars Jedis," BBC Science Focus Magazine, posted August 23, 2023, accessed August 12, 2024, https://www.sciencefocus.com/the-human-body/ahsoka-jedi-mind-tricks

Gerry Doyle, Mariano Zafra, "The Air War Over Ukraine," Reuters.com, posted December 14, 2023, accessed August 12, 2024, https://www.reuters.com

James Alder, "What is an audible in football?" Liveaboutdot.com, posted April 7, 2018, accessed August 13, 2024, https://www.liveabout.com/about-football-glossary-audible-1333801

Frank Viola, "Rethinking "Quiet Time", Frank Viola Beyond Evangelical, accessed August 13, 2024, www.frankviola.org

Alicia Britt Chole, *The Night is Normal,* (Carol Stream, IL: Tyndale House Publishers, Inc., 2023), p 107-108

John Nemo, "What a NASA janitor can teach us about living a bigger life," The Business Journals, posted December 23, 2014, accessed August 15, 2024, www.bizjournals.com

Booker T Washington, "Up From Slavery: An Autobiography," Literaturepage.com, accessed August 15, 2024, https://www.literaturepage.com/read/upfromslavery-39.html

"Parolee and Probation Law," Criminal Law Center, accessed September 6, 2024, www.justia.com

Robert J. Morgan, *Then Sings My Soul*, (Nashville, TN: Thomas Nelson Publishing, 2003) pages 14, 80, 112, 130, 132, 184, 192, 284

Chris Crouch, "The one thing in your life that matters most," Knoxville News Sentinel, posted February 2, 2019, accessed September 13, 2024, www.knownews.com

Nancy DeMoss Wolgemuth, *The Quiet Place, Daily Devotional Readings,* (Chicago IL: Moody Publishers, 2012), September 14th, "Full vs. Empty," November 21st, "Seeking His Pleasure," November 23rd, "Now Thank We All Our God"

Deborah Serani PSY.D., "If it Bleeds, It Leads: Understanding Fear-Based Media," Psychology Today, posted June 7, 2011, accessed September 17, 2024, https://www.psychologytoday.com/us/blog/two-takes-depression/201106/if-it-bleeds-it-leads-understanding-fear-based-media

Tim Kight, "Chronos vs. Kairos," A Call to Excellence, posted February 27, 2023, accessed September 24, 202https://www.acalltoexcellence.com/chronos-vs-kairos/

Lauren Hodges Ed.D., "What John Wayne and C.S. Lewis have to say about Courage (and what we can do to get more of it)," LinkedIn, posted April 5, 2019, accessed October 2, 2024, https://www.linkedin.com/pulse/what-john-wayne-cs-lewis-have-say-courage-we-can-do-hodges-ed-d-

"Psalm 91: The Soldier's Song," Museum of the Bible, posted May 3, 2021, accessed October 15, 2024, https://www.museumofthebible.org/book-minute/psalm-91

Dan Jones, "Psalm 91 and the Miracle of Dunkirk," Kinship Radio, posted March 25, 2020, accessed October 15, 2024, https://kinshipradio.org/home/psalm-91-and-the-miracle-of-dunkirk/

Jim Davidson, "Psalm 91: God's Shield of Protection!" Banner News, posted November 2, 2018, accessed October 15, 2024, https://www.magnoliabannernews.com/news/2018/nov/02/psalm-91-gods-shield-protection/

"Tales of Courage: Corrie Ten Boom, Tales of Courage Podcast and Blog, posted February 15, 2021, accessed October 15, 2024,https://www.talesofcourage.com/blog/corrie-ten-boom

Emily Brooks, "Waiting For Your Ticket: The Courage of Corrie Ten Boom," Emilybrookswriter.com, accessed October 15, 2024, https://emilybrookswriter.com/2022/07/24/waiting-for-your-ticket-the-courage-of-corrie-ten-boom/

Dan Button, "Making Seeing Eyes Blind – Tributed to Brother Andrew," Gateway Theology School, posted November 30, 2022, accessed 10/16/2024, https://gtstheology.org/make-seeing-eyes-blind-tribute-to-brother-andrew/

Margot Morrell, Stephanie Capparell, *Shackleton's Way: Leadership Lessons from the Great Antarctic Explorer,* (New York, NY: Penguin Group, 2001)

Kieran Mulvaney, "The Stunning Survival Story of Ernest Shackleton and his Endurance Crew," History.com, updated May 2, 2024, accessed November 11, 2024, https://www.history.com/news/shackleton-endurance-survival

Joyce Vollmer Brown, *Courageous Christians, Devotional Stories For Family Reading,* (Chicago IL: Moody Publishers, 2000), pages 11, 21, 25, 27, 39, 57, 97, 101, 109, 115, 127, 145

"Reflections on Charles Colson," Blackaby Ministries International, posted on May 8, 2012, accessed November 21, 2024, https://blackaby.org/reflections-on-chuck-colson/

Karisa You, "The Prayer Life of George Muller," Sola Network, posted September 6, 2022, accessed December 9, 2024, https://sola.network/article/the-prayer-life-of-george-muller/

Susan Verstraete, "Trusting God in Tragedy: Elizabeth Prentiss," posted 2011, accessed December 11, 2024, https://bulletininserts.org/trusting-god-in-tragedy-elizabeth-prentiss/

"Bethany's Story," accessed December 17, 2024, https://bethanyhamiltonsoulsurferproject.weebly.com/

S. Pangambam, "The Opportunity of Adversity: Aimee Mullins," The Sinju Post, posted November 8, 2019, accessed December 17, 2024, https://singjupost.com/the-opportunity-of-adversity-aimee-mullins-full-transcript/?singlepage=1

Marjie Schaefer, Flourish Through The Word, posted 2017, accessed December 18, 2024, https://static1.squarespace.com/static/6644000b712a356f4203564c/t/66d8e3531d15ad1b5c65066a/1725490003486/LG-Week-2-Be-Brave-2-2021_1_.pdf

Mary A. Kassian, *Growing Grateful,* (Nashville, TN; Thomas Nelson Publishing, 2020), pages 41-42

Brene Brown, *Daring Greatly* (New York, NY: Gotham Books, 2012)

"How to Balance and Stay on a Gymnastics Beam?" Gymnastgem, updated April 25, 2024, accessed January 23, 2024, https://gymnastgem.com/balance-on-beam

Dr. Dean Borgman, "Courage for Troubled Times, The Surprising Power of Hymn Poetry," Emannuel Gospel Center, posted July 24, 2019, accessed January 26, 2025, www.egc.org

Mysia Haight, "95+ C.S. Lewis quotes about love, life, faith, bravery, and friendship," posted January 31, 2021, accessed January 26, 2025, https://www.audible.com/blog/quotes-cs-lewis,

Free Bible Study Resources

The vision for *Flourish Through The Word* comes from 1 Chronicles 16:23-24:

"Let the whole earth sing to the Lord! Each day proclaim the good news that He saves. Publish His glorious deeds among the nations. Tell everyone about the amazing things He does."

Our vision is to see Flourish's resources (workbooks, books, and videos) published and made available for all individuals and churches of every nation in their own language at no cost to them (Daniel 7:14; Matthew 24:14).

Flourish will pay for the following:
- **Printing**
- **Translation**
- **Shipping**

Why free?

Because we believe the Bible alone is *"living and powerful, and sharper than any two-edged sword, piercing even to the division of soul and spirit, and of joints and marrow, and is a discerner of the thoughts and intents of the heart"* (Hebrews 4:12), and that *"His Word will never return void"* (Isaiah 55:11). Our prayer and desire is to see each person in every tribe and nation experience the power of God's Word for themselves through their personal study of it.

So, if you need resources for your church or Bible study, please go to

https://www.flourishthroughtheword.com/bible-study-resources

Fill out a request for resources, and upon approval, *Flourish* will do the rest.

May God bless you and those you influence as together you study His Word!

Based on Galatians chapter 5, this 6-week Bible study will take you on a deep study of the fruit of the Holy Spirit.

A 5-week Bible study that features the conversation of Jesus with His disciples in the gospel of John chapters 14, 15, and 16.

A five-week journey on grace, truth, the Holy Spirit, and our identity, starting with the Gospel of John.

Spend four weeks on biblical principles of friendship, exploring commitment, communication, and community through Scripture.

Explore 1 Peter, focusing on faith, hope, love, and practical Christian living through a five-week personal study.

The letter of 2 Peter focuses on spiritual disciplines and intentional growth through Jesus' provision for living in truth.

A six-week study on how God's Word transforms us, guiding us to flourish spiritually and joyfully.

Learn how investing in others and recognizing their worth through biblical disciple-making principles is a life-giving key.

BY MARJIE SCHAEFER

A seven-week study inviting deeper relationship with God through biblical stories, declarations, and gratitude journaling.

BY MARJIE SCHAEFER

This five-week study in James focuses on practical wisdom and spiritual growth through daily biblical reflection.

by Marjie Schaefer

Explore how personal stories fit into God's Kingdom by studying the book of Habakkuk and the life of David.

This five-week study examines biblical stories of faith and courage, offering encouragement and guidance for facing fear.

This six-week study highlights the bravery of Abraham, Mary, the mother of Jesus, Peter and John, Paul and Silas, King David, and the woman at the well.

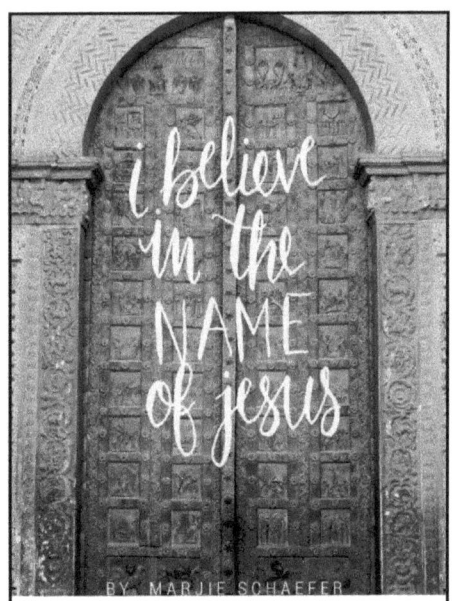

A study of the seven "I Am" statements of Jesus, exploring their significance and impact.

Walk through the book of Ephesians, focusing on Christ's majesty and practical daily living through Paul's biblical prayers and teachings.

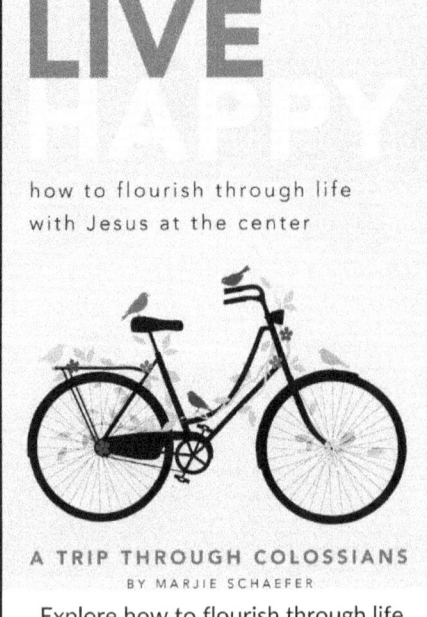

Explore how to flourish through life with Jesus at the center, focusing on joy, renewal, and practical teachings from the book of Colossians.

A four-week study of Philippians,
teaching how to find true joy through
gratitude and knowing Jesus as we rise
above our circumstances by grace.

Other Devotional Readings from Steve & Marjie Schaefer

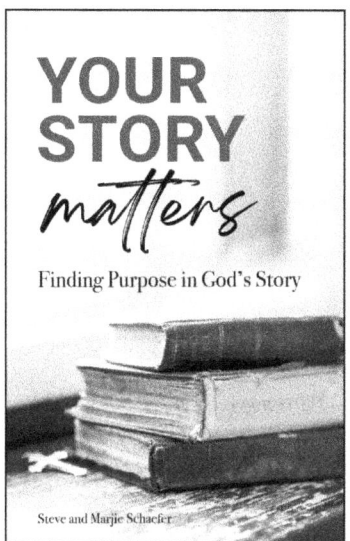